99 Fascinating Heroes and Villains
of the Bible

museum of the Bible

BOOKS

Executive Editorial Team
Allen Quine
Wayne Hastings
Jeana Ledbetter
Byron Williamson

Development Editor
Randy Southern

Managing Editor
Christopher D. Hudson

Senior Editors
Jennifer Stair
Cynthia Tucker

Worthy Editorial
Kyle Olund
Leeanna Nelson

Design & Page Layout
Hudson Bible

Cover Design
Matt Smartt,
Smartt Guys design

99 Fascinating Heroes and Villains of the Bible
© 2018 Museum of the Bible, Inc., Washington, DC 20014

Published by Worthy Publishing Group, a division of Worthy Media, Inc. in association with Museum of the Bible.

ISBN-10: 1945470364
ISBN-13: 978-1945470363

Cataloging-in-Publication Data is on file with the Library of Congress.

Unless otherwise indicated, Scripture quotations are from the ESV® Bible (The Holy Bible, English Standard Version®), copyright © 2001 by Crossway, a publishing ministry of Good News Publishers. Used by permission. All rights reserved.

Produced with the assistance of Hudson Bible (www.HudsonBible.com).

Cover image: Art Directors & TRIP / Alamy Stock Photo

Printed in the USA

1 2 3 4 5 6 7 8 9 LAKE 23 22 21 20 19 18

museum of the Bible
BOOKS

WORTHY®
PUBLISHING

Introduction

99 Fascinating Heroes and Villains of the Bible

Introduction

One of the features of the Bible that lend it credibility as a book of history is its honesty in presenting its heroes. It doesn't attempt to present flawed human beings as flawless heroes. It simply tells the whole truth, whether flattering or not.

In classic literature, the hero often made a tragic mistake and then died without the opportunity to right his wrongs, but the Bible leaves room for repentance and restoration Biblical heroes are those who repent of their sins and depend on God as their source of strength. The heroes of the Bible are not heroes because they are perfect. They are not heroes because of their innate abilities or talents. They are heroes because God molded flawed individuals into people who could make a difference for his kingdom. This is a great source of encouragement to Christians, all of whom are flawed, but are called and loved by God all the same. If the adulterous David could be considered Israel's greatest king; if the deceitful Jacob could become the father of the Israelites; if the murderer Saul of Tarsus could become Paul, God's chief apostle, there is hope for you—there is hope for me.

The characters presented in this book are listed in biblical order according to tradition. Their order is not meant to be taken as an authoritative statement or the final word on their chronology. Many may disagree, and that is ok; this is merely one approach.

Marble statue of Agony of Cain from Bible.
Hermitage in St. Petersburg, Russia

01 Cain
(Genesis 4)

Genesis 4 is a chapter of firsts: the first conception, the first birth, the first sacrifice, the first sibling rivalry, and the first murder.

Cain was the firstborn son of Adam and Eve; Abel was the second. Cain was a worker of the ground; Abel was a keeper of sheep. Both brothers offered sacrifices to God. Cain offered the fruits of his farming labor, while Abel offered his firstborn sheep.

For reasons the Bible doesn't make clear, the LORD had no regard for Cain and his offering, but he had regard for Abel and his offering. The LORD sees Cain's anger and tells him that if he does well, he will be accepted. These incidents seem to have triggered something in Cain.

Cain became jealous, and then he grew angry . . . and then he turned murderous. He killed Abel in a field. According to Genesis 4:9, the LORD asked Cain, "Where is your brother Abel?" Cain's reply has become infamous: "I do not know; am I my brother's keeper?"

For Abel's murder, Cain was condemned to be a fugitive and a wanderer, and the earth would no longer yield itself to his work.

**Marble statue of Abel from Bible.
Hermitage in St. Petersburg, Russia**

02 Noah
(Genesis 6–8)

The Bible says that "Noah was a righteous man, blameless in his generation," that he "walked with God," and that he "found favor in the eyes of the LORD" (Genesis 6:8–9). Consider the tasks to which he was called.

In preparation for the deluge to come, Noah's God instructed him to:

* construct an ark of gopher wood 450 long, 75 feet wide, and 45 feet high,
* install three decks, a door, various rooms, and a roof,
* coat the entire vessel with pitch—inside and out,
* lead at least two of every kind of animal (male and female) into the ark to be kept alive,
* gather every kind of food for the journey, and
* coax his family into the ark.

The list of things that could have gone wrong is virtually endless. According to Genesis 7:6, Noah was nearly 600 years old when the flood occurred. God outlines to Noah how he was to build an ark made of cypress or gopher wood, with a roof and various decks, rooms, and a door in its side, and sealed with pitch to be watertight. So according to Genesis 6:22, Noah "did all that God commanded him".

His reward was a place for him and his family on his own vessel when the flood described in Genesis 7 began. Inside the ark, Noah likely drew from reserves of patience, ingenuity, and resourcefulness that he didn't know he possessed in order to keep his family safe, sane, and focused.

Noah also had many animals to care for. He found himself the caretaker of countless species facing extinction. The Bible tells us his job was to "keep them alive" for as long as it took the floodwaters to recede.

Noah and his passengers disembarked after spending more than a year on the ark. The Bible says that God blessed Noah and his family, and said to them, "Be fruitful and multiply on the earth" (Genesis 8:13–19).

Afterward, Noah built an altar to the LORD, and offered burnt offerings to God.

03
Job
(Job 1–42)

Job had everything—wealth, possessions, family, and excellent health. And then, through no fault of his own, he had nothing. The Job narrative suggests that this man—whom the text describes as righteous—was an unwitting participant in a cosmic challenge between God and "the accuser".

The LORD held up Job as a model: "a blameless and upright man who fears God and turns away from evil" (Job 1:8). Satan countered that if Job's blessings were taken away, his faithfulness and righteousness would disappear with them. the LORD gave "the accuser" permission to torment Job.

The torment started when messengers informed Job that all his flocks had been killed or stolen. His wealth was gone. Another messenger brought news that the house of Job's oldest son had collapsed, killing him and all his brothers and sisters during a family gathering. His children were dead. Through all of that, Job did not accuse God or sin.

The torment continued. Though his life was spared, Job was attacked with painful boils all over his body, from the bottom of his feet to the top of his head. His health was shot.

His wife said to him, "Do you still hold fast your integrity? Curse God and die." But he said to her, "You speak as one of the foolish women

would speak. Shall we receive good from God, and shall we not receive evil?" In all this Job did not sin with his lips. (Job 2:9–10)

His friends told Job that he was getting what he deserved—that he was being punished by his God for something he had done. His sources of comfort and encouragement abandoned him.

Job protested his innocence, with no success.

Job struggled mightily with his situation, arguing with his friends and trying to reconcile his suffering and losses with what he believed about God. He pleaded for someone to serve as a mediator between him and God (Job 9:32-33), someone to get the answers that eluded him. At one point, he begged God to send him to Sheol, the place of the dead (Job 14:13).

The Bible records that through it all, Job spoke what was right about the LORD and maintained his righteousness in the eyes of God. In the end, God rewarded his faithfulness. According to Job 42:10–17, the LORD restored Job's health and gave him a long life. He bestowed on Job twice as much wealth and possessions as he had before. He also blessed Job with more children—seven sons and three daughters.

Job and his three friends. Drawn by Gustave Doré, French artist, b. January 6, 1832 – d. January 23, 1883. Engraved by J. Regnier.

04

Abram, Abraham
(Genesis 12–23)

The Life & Journey of Abraham

1. Abraham leaves Ur (Gen. 11:1)

2. Abraham travels through Babylon

3. Abraham called by God in Haran (Gen. 12:1-3)

4. Abraham arrives in the Promised Land, Shechem (Gen. 12:5)

5. Abraham moves to Egypt (Gen. 12:10-20)

6. Abraham returns to the Promised Land, Hebron (Gen. 13:1)

Now the Lord said to Abram, "Go from your country and your kindred and your father's house to the land that I will show you.

(Genesis 12:1)

Those were the instructions Abram received from the Lord. Abraham didn't hesitate: "So Abram went" (12:4). With his wife, Sarai, and his nephew, Lot, he set out for the unknown. Along the way, the Lord made a covenant with him, modifying his name to Abraham and promising to make a great nation from his offspring (15; 17)—even though he and his wife, now called Sarah, were well past childbearing age.

On arriving in Canaan, Abraham and Lot agreed to go their separate ways (13). Abraham gave his nephew first choice as to where he would settle. Lot chose the well-watered Jordan Valley near the city of Sodom. Afterward the Lord had Abraham look "northward and southward and eastward and westward," beyond Lot's choice, and promised that "all the land that you see I will give to you and to your offspring forever" (13:14). Abraham then walked through the land, its length and its breadth, and settled near the oaks of Mamre at Hebron, where he built an altar to the Lord.

Years later, the Lord told Abraham that he was going to destroy the cities of Sodom and Gomorrah because

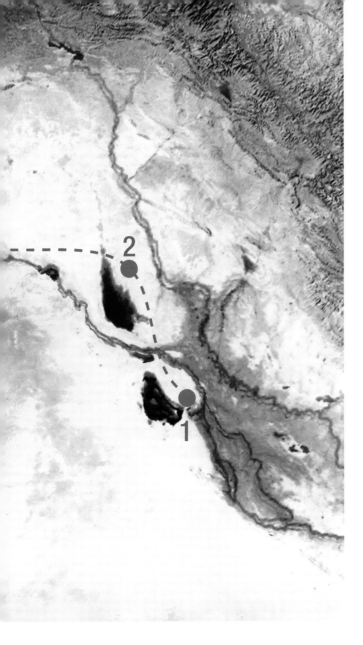

thirty, then twenty, and finally ten. Had anyone else ever approached the LORD with such boldness? Unfortunately, not even ten righteous people could be found in Sodom and Gomorrah, so both cities were destroyed.

Abraham first fathered Ishmael, with his wife's servant Hagar, then Isaac, with his wife Sarah.

Isaac was a young man when God tested Abraham and told him to "Take your son, your only son Isaac, whom you love" (22:2). Abraham didn't negotiate this time. He prepared for the journey, went with Isaac, prepared an altar, and laid Isaac on top of it.

In Genesis 22, the captivating story continues:

Then Abraham reached out his hand and took the knife to slaughter his son. But the angel of the LORD called to him from heaven and said, "Abraham, Abraham!" And he said, "Here I am." He said, "Do not lay your hand on the boy or do anything to him, for now I know that you fear God, seeing you have not withheld your son, your only son, from me." And Abraham lifted up his eyes and looked, and behold, behind him was a ram, caught in a thicket by his horns. And Abraham went and took the ram and offered it up as a burnt offering instead of his son. So Abraham called the name of that place, "The LORD will provide"; as it is said to this day, "On the mount of the LORD it shall be provided." . . . "By myself I have sworn, declares the LORD, because you have done this and have not with- held your son, your only son, I will surely bless you, and I will surely multiply your offspring as the stars of heaven and as the sand that is on the seashore. And your offspring shall possess the gate of his enemies, and in your offspring shall all the nations of the earth be blessed, because you have obeyed my voice" (Genesis 22:10–14, 16–18).

of the wickedness of the people there. With the utmost humility and respect, Abraham urged the LORD to consider the people in those cities who weren't wicked.

"Suppose there are fifty righteous within the city," he said to the LORD. "Will you then sweep away the place and not spare it for the fifty righteous who are in it?" (Genesis 18:24).

The LORD said yes, he would spare it; so Abraham grew bolder.

"Suppose five of the fifty righteous are lacking. Will you destroy the whole city for lack of five?" (Genesis 18:28).

The LORD said yes again. Abraham's intercessory countdown brought the number down to forty, then

05 Melchizedek
(Genesis 14)

Melchizedek stained glass, St. John the Baptist Church, Mathon, Herefordshire, England, UK

Melchizedek stands as one of the most mysterious figures in the Bible. Genesis 14 identifies him as the king of Salem (an ancient name for Jerusalem), as well as a "priest of God Most High"—the same God Abraham served.

Abraham encountered Melchizedek on his way back from a victory in battle. Five kings had combined their forces to attack the cities of Sodom and Gomorrah and take away their people and possessions. Among the captives were Abraham's nephew Lot and his family.

Abraham assembled his own fighting force of 318 men, "his trained men, born in his house" (14:14), to rescue the people and retrieve their possessions. He was returning home with the spoils when Melchizedek came out to meet him. The encounter was short yet profound.

The king of Salem gave Abraham bread and wine, as well as a blessing from "God Most High" whom they both worshiped. Abraham gave Melchizedek one-tenth of all his captured prizes—a tithe for a priest he considered worthy to receive it.

Melchizedek blesses Abram
(Genesis 14, 18-20) - Illustration

Psalm 110

Psalm 110, a psalm of David, refers to Melchizedek. A psalm identified as one of the "messianic psalms," the text says:

The LORD says to my Lord:
 "Sit at my right hand,
 until I make your enemies your footstool." . . .
 The Lord has sworn
 and will not change his mind,
 "You are a priest forever
 after the order of Melchizedek."

In the New Testament, the writer of Hebrews cites Psalm 110:4 in describing the priesthood of Jesus, asserting he was "designated by God a high priest after the order of Melchizedek" (Hebrews 5:5, 10).

06 The People of Sodom and Gomorrah
(Genesis 18–19)

Abraham risked incurring the wrath of God to plead on behalf of the people of Sodom. Abraham learned that the LORD planned to destroy the city because of its wickedness. The concerned patriarch is described as carefully negotiating with the LORD to spare the city if ten righteous people were found there.

The narrative of Genesis 19 suggests that the people of Sodom were considerably less concerned about their standing before Abraham's God than Abraham was. Abraham's nephew, Lot, lived in the city. According to Genesis 19, Lot was sitting just within gate of Sodom when he saw two men approaching. The men, it turns out, were angels. Evening was falling, and Lot strongly encouraged them to spend the night in the safety of his home.

A respectful host, Lot prepared a feast for his guests. Before they could all retire for the night, however, they encountered very real danger.

The men of Sodom, both young and old, surrounded Lot's house and demanded that he send his visitors out "that we may know them," a way of saying have sexual relations with them. Lot pleaded with the men not to do such a wicked thing—and he even offered his virgin daughters to the crowd of men instead. The men of Sodom grew angry and impatient. They approached the house to break down Lot's door to get to the visitors inside. Before they could, the angels struck the assailants blind.

Then the angels urged Lot and his family to leave Sodom immediately—and not to look back. Lot and his family escaped the city as fire and sulfur fell from heaven, killing everyone and utterly destroying the city.

Lot and his daughter, coloured woodcut by Jost Amman, 'Biblia. Die ganze Heylige Schrifft teutsch', printed by Sigmund Feyerabend and Georg Raben, Frankfurt am Main, 1564, private collection.

07 Sarai, Sarah
(Genesis 16, 18, 21)

Sarai, the wife of Abram, thought she understood the plan. The God of her people had promised to make a great nation of her husband's descendants. But there was a problem: Sarai was unable to conceive. When God made his promise to Abram, Sara was seventy-five years of age—obviously too old to hope that she would be able to bear children. The only other female in their household was her maidservant Hagar, who was of childbearing age.

Sarai thought God's plan must be for Abram to conceive an heir with Hagar. So Sarai told Abram to go to Hagar, and Hagar got pregnant. Suddenly, the dynamics of the household changed. Hagar realized that she was giving Abram the child Sarai couldn't provide, and she began to treat Sarai with contempt. Sarai responded by becoming abusive toward Hagar. The dysfunction continued for years.

One day a trio of visitors arrived at Abram's tent with a message: Sarai, now to be called Sarah, was going to give birth to a son. She was ninety years old. Abram, now to be called Abraham and who was 100, would father the son.

When she heard this, Sarah couldn't help but laugh.

Her laughter turned to amazement and joy when she became pregnant and gave birth to a son that God had named Isaac (Genesis 17:19)

The Sister-Wife

Sarah was known for her extraordinary beauty. She was so beautiful that it made her husband fearful. When the family traveled through foreign lands, Abraham feared that the rulers of those lands would kill him and take Sarah for themselves. so he instructed her to tell people that she was his sister. Technically, that wasn't a lie. Sarah was Abraham's half-sister, the daughter of Abraham's father, Terah.

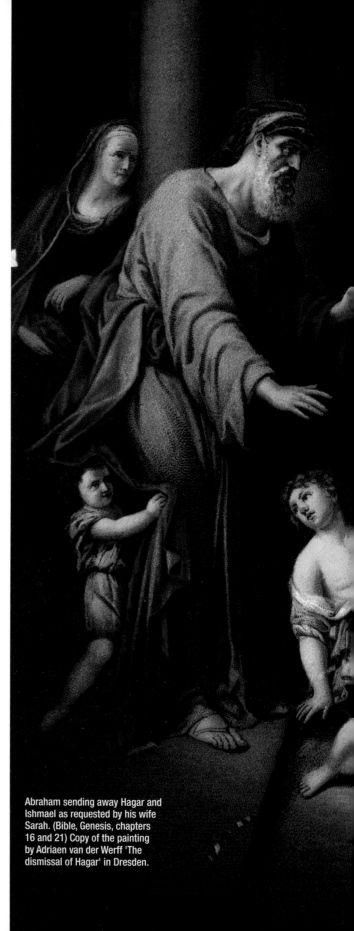

Abraham sending away Hagar and Ishmael as requested by his wife Sarah. (Bible, Genesis, chapters 16 and 21) Copy of the painting by Adriaen van der Werff 'The dismissal of Hagar' in Dresden.

08 Hagar
(Genesis 16, 21)

It was a recipe for trouble from the start: two women raising sons fathered by the same man in the same household. One woman was his wife; the other was her handmaiden.

Hagar, the handmaiden, had not asked to be put in such a position. When Abraham's wife Sarah believed herself to be infertile, Hagar seemed to be the only hope for giving Abraham an heir. So Hagar bore his son Ishmael. When Sarah later gave birth to Isaac, Hagar and Ishmael's importance dropped dramatically.

As the two sons got older, it became apparent that this blended family approach was not working. The breaking point came when Sarah caught Ishmael mocking Isaac. This, plus her concern that Hagar would take Isaac's inheritance, caused her to demand that Abraham banish Hagar and her son Ishmael to the desert wilderness.

Abraham eventually agreed to Sarah's plan after God tells him that he will also make Ishmael the father of a nation "because he is your offspring" (21:13). So he gave Hagar and Ishmael a supply of bread and water and sent them away to an uncertain fate.

The water ran out quickly, and so did Hagar's hope. She made Ishmael as comfortable as possible in the shade of a bush and then found a place for herself "the distance of a bowshot" (21:16), which is about 50–100 yards away. She couldn't bear to watch her son die.

Hagar wept. And then an angel of God spoke from heaven: "What troubles you, Hagar? Fear not, for God has heard the voice of the boy where he is. Up! Lift up the boy, and hold him fast with your hand, for I will make him into a great nation" (21:17–18).

Hagar noticed a nearby well that she hadn't seen before. She filled her container with water and gave Ishmael a drink. That moment marked a dramatic turn in their fortunes. Hagar and Ishmael thrived in their seemingly inhospitable surroundings. Hagar found an Egyptian woman for Ishmael to marry, and they all settled in the desert wilderness of Paran.

09 Isaac
(Genesis 22)

Isaac was a young man when he and his father set out for the land of Moriah (a region of modern-day Jerusalem) to offer a sacrifice. His father, Abraham, was well over 100 years old.

Obediently, Isaac followed his father to a distant land. He raised no objections when Abraham told the servants who had traveled with them not to approach the sacrifice area. Isaac carried the wood for the burnt offering from the caravan to the place of the sacrifice.

Isaac asked a single question: "My father! . . . Where is the lamb for a burnt offering?" And he accepted Abraham's vague reply: "God will provide for himself the lamb for a burnt offering, my son" (Genesis 22:7–8). And onward, together, they went.

The Bible doesn't relate Isaac's response when his father laid him on the altar he had built. We might think that Isaac would have pulled away when his father started to tie him up. He could have overpowered the old man. He could have run away. He could have screamed for help. Instead, he allowed his father to lay him on the wood as the sacrifice for the burnt offering. Then, Abraham took the knife to slaughter his son.

In the Genesis account, an angel of the LORD stopped Abraham before he sacrificed his son. Abraham was commended for his obedience and reverence of God, and rewarded for his sacrificial faith. Isaac later fathered twins, Esau and Jacob, becoming the grandfather of Jacob's children, who later made up the twelve tribes of Israel.

Abraham sacrificing Isaac

10 Jacob
(Genesis 25–29)

Jacob was the second-born of twin boys in a culture where the firstborn son received a double portion of his family's inheritance, plus a special blessing from his father. One day when Jacob's older twin brother, Esau, returned from a hunt famished, Jacob offered his brother a bowl of lentil stew in exchange for Esau's birthright. Later, with the help of his mother, Rebekah, Jacob tricked Esau out of his special blessing as well.

Esau, who was left with nothing, vowed to kill Jacob after their father died. Rebekah learned of his plan and sent Jacob to live with her brother, Laban, in Haran, a distant land. Up to this point, it seems Jacob did not have a personal relationship with the God of Israel. However, during his travels, God appeared to him in a dream and said:

> "I am the Lord, the God of Abraham your father and the God of Isaac. The land on which you lie I will give to you and to your offspring. Your offspring shall be like the dust of the earth, and you shall spread abroad to the west and to the east and to the north and to the south, and in you and your offspring shall all the families of the earth be blessed. Behold, I am with you and will keep you wherever you go, and will bring you back to this land. For I will not leave you until I have done what I have promised you." (Genesis 28:13–15)

When Jacob woke up, he exclaimed, "Surely the Lord is in this place, and I did not know it. . . . How awesome is this place! This is none other than the house of God, and this is the gate of heaven" (Genesis 28:16–17). He named that place Bethel and set up a pillar to honor God. Before leaving, he vowed that if indeed God stayed with him and brought him back safely to the land of his father, he would serve him faithfully.

Once settled in with Laban's family, Jacob fell in love with Laban's younger daughter Rachel. Laban agreed to allow Jacob to marry Rachel in exchange for seven years of labor. Seven years later, on Jacob's wedding day, Laban tricked Jacob. He substituted his older daughter Leah for Rachel. In order to marry Rachel too, Jacob had to work seven *more* years for Laban. The deceiver had just learned what it felt like to be deceived.

Genesis 32 records another meeting of Jacob with God as he traveled homeward with his family. Jacob wrestled all night with "a man" and insisted on being blessed by him before he would let him go. The mystery assailant concedes somewhat and declares that Jacob would be called "Israel" because he had "striven with God and with men, and . . . prevailed." Jacob names the place Peniel (which means "the face of God") saying, "I have seen God face to face, and yet my life has been delivered" (Genesis 32:28–30). Subsequently, God renames Jacob "Israel" as foreshadowed by his mysterious assailant (Genesis 35:10).

The Genesis narratives relate that Jacob's life continued to be fraught with difficulties, realized through his relationships with his sons. But he had encountered God, and the Jacob who had come to Laban wasn't the same as the Jacob who left. This is demonstrated most clearly in Genesis 33, when Jacob sought out his brother Esau and made amends for the way he had deceived his older brother. Even so rather than going to the land of Seir with Esau as he said he would, Jacob went to Succoth, finally settling at Shechem.

According to the biblical narratives, Jacob became the father of the twelve tribes of Israel, flawed indeed, but blessed by and chosen by God all the same.

11 Leah
(Genesis 29)

In Olympic winner terms, Leah was the silver medal at her own wedding.

Leah began her married life through an incredible deception by her father. Jacob wanted to marry Leah's beautiful younger sister Rachel. In fact, Jacob had worked seven years for her father, Laban, for that very privilege. But Laban crossed him. He tricked Jacob into marrying Leah instead and told him that he had to work another seven years in order to also marry his beloved Rachel.

Genesis 29:30–31 summarizes Jacob's feelings for his first wife: "he loved Rachel more than Leah . . . the LORD saw that Leah was hated." Nevertheless, she was a faithful wife and bore him six sons. She couldn't change her husband's feelings toward her, but she could—and did—make herself an integral part of his life.

Leah may have been Jacob's second choice as wife, but the Bible indicates that God showed her favor. "When the LORD saw that Leah was hated, he opened her womb, but Rachel was barren" (Genesis 29:31).

Leah's ability to bear children—especially sons—set her apart from her sister Rachel, who was thought to be barren. Many historians relate that in biblical times, a woman who was unable to bear children for her husband was considered cursed by God and held in great shame. In all, Leah gave birth to six sons—half of the twelve tribes of Israel—and one daughter. Her third son, Levi, was the forefather of Israel's line of priests. Her fourth son, Judah, was the forefather of Jesus.

12 Rachel
(Genesis 29-31)

VATICAN: Jacob meeting Rachel & Leah
(6th Loggie vault), antique print 1872.

For Jacob, it was love at first sight.

Jacob's parents had sent him to stay with his uncle Laban for a while, and he fell in love with Rachel, one of Laban's daughters. Her older sister was named Leah. The Bible describes them this way: "Leah's eyes were weak, but Rachel was beautiful in form and appearance" (Genesis 29:17). That sentence sets the stage for an ongoing rivalry between the sisters, due to the difficult position their father placed them in.

Jacob loved Rachel so much that he agreed to work for Laban seven years in exchange for her hand in marriage. However, when it was time for them to marry, Laban gave Jacob Leah instead of Rachel. His excuse was that the oldest daughter had to be married first. And he assured Jacob he could still marry Rachel the following week….if he agreed to work for another seven years.

Jacob's love for Rachel knew no bounds, and he agreed to another seven years of labor. However, in arranging for the sisters to marry the same man, Laban had created a tense state of affairs. Genesis 29:30 says Jacob loved Rachel more than he loved Leah, but that didn't make Rachel's life any easier.

Genesis 29:31 explains the situation: "When the LORD saw that Leah was hated, he opened her womb, but Rachel was barren." Not only did Rachel have to share the husband who should have been hers alone, she now had to watch her sister have children while she could have none. Thus began a battle between the sisters to produce more children. Rachel gave Jacob her servant Bilhah to have children for her (a custom during that time). When Leah stopped having children, she gave Jacob her servant as well.

Eventually, "God remembered Rachel, and God listened to her and opened her womb. She conceived and bore a son and said, 'God has taken away my reproach.' And she called his name Joseph, saying, 'May the LORD add to me another son!' (Genesis 30:22–24).

When Jacob was finally ready to leave Laban's household with his family, he consulted Leah and Rachel. They responded, "Is there any portion or inheritance left to us in our father's house? Are we not regarded by him as foreigners? For he has sold us, and he has indeed devoured our money. All the wealth that God has taken away from our father belongs to us and to our children. Now then, whatever God has said to you, do" (Genesis 31:14–16).

But before they left, Rachel stole some of her father's idols and hid them in her camel's saddle. Some scholars believe that possession of these idols indicated a legal claim to an estate.

Laban chased down the caravan and searched everyone. When the time came to search Rachel's camel, she refused to climb down, claiming, "Let not my lord be angry that I cannot rise before you, for the way of women is upon me" (Genesis 31:35).

Sometime later, God did honor Rachel's request for another son, but her labor was a difficult one and her life was departing just as she was bringing new life into the world. With her last breath, she named her son Ben-oni (son of my sorrow), but Jacob changed his name to Benjamin (son of my right hand). Rachel was buried on the way to Bethlehem, where the family had been heading.

In the New Testament when Herod orders the death of all the boys in Bethlehem two years old and younger, the Gospel writer identifies these children with Rachel and her own loss, referencing a quote from the prophet Jeremiah:

A voice was heard in Ramah,
weeping and loud lamentation,
Rachel weeping for her children;
she refused to be comforted,
because they are no more. (Matthew 2:18)

13 Joseph and Joseph's Brothers
(Genesis 37–50)

Giovanni Andrea de Ferrari - 'Joseph's Coat Brought to Jacob', oil on canvas, c. 1640, El Paso Museum of Art

Jacob's family is a study in dysfunction. Jacob had twelve sons by four different women—two wives and two maidservants. The ever-shifting power struggles among the women created rivalries among their sons.

Joseph was Jacob's eleventh son—and his first son with Rachel, the love of his life. Rachel died giving birth to Benjamin, Joseph's younger brother, so Joseph represented Jacob's last fond memories of Rachel. He became Jacob's favorite son.

Jacob lavished attention and gifts on Joseph, including a richly ornamented robe that drew the ire of Joseph's older brothers. Purposefully or not, Joseph did quite a bit to stoke that ire. He brought a bad report of them to his father while they were tending sheep. Worst of all, he told them his dreams that one day his father and brothers would bow down to him.

That was the last straw for Joseph's older brothers. Sometime later, when he went to check on them in the field, they decided to rid themselves of their younger brother once and for all. After Reuben persuaded his brothers not to kill Joseph, they threw him into a waterless pit. When they saw a caravan of Ishmaelites headed to Egypt, they sold him to them. Then they tore Joseph's special robe, killed a goat, and smeared its blood on the garment. They took the robe back to their father and let him think the worst about Joseph's fate. The brothers' deception resulted in Jacob weeping and mourning Joseph for many years.

Meanwhile in Egypt, Joseph had been sold to an Egyptian government official named Potiphar. Later, after Potiphar's wife falsely accused Joseph of trying to seduce her, Joseph was thrown in prison. But he refused to be beaten down by his circumstances. We

After being sold into slavery, Joseph travelled by caravan to Egypt.

are told that "the Lord was with Joseph and showed him steadfast love and gave him favor in the sight of the keeper of the prison" (Genesis 39:21). Before long, the warden put all the prisoners under Joseph's supervision.

One day the king's cupbearer and baker arrived as prisoners. Both men were troubled by dreams filled with symbolism. Joseph volunteered to interpret their dreams: "Do not interpretations belong to God? Please tell them to me" (Genesis 40:8). He told the cupbearer that he would be restored to his old position in three days. He told the baker that he would be executed in three days. He proved to be right in both cases.

Joseph asked the cupbearer to put in a good word for him with Pharaoh. But the cupbearer forgot about Joseph—for two years—until Pharaoh himself had some troubling dreams.

No one could interpret the dreams, so the cupbearer remembered his prison experience and suggested Joseph. Pharaoh sent for Joseph immediately and told him his dreams, which Joseph interpreted on the spot, crediting God with the interpretation: "It is not in me; God will give Pharaoh a favorable answer" (Genesis 41:16). He told Pharaoh that Egypt would experience seven years of abundance, followed by seven years of famine. He advised the king to appoint a wise leader to oversee preparations for the famine—to make sure that one-fifth of the grain collected during the years of abundance was put into long-term storage. Pharaoh gave the job to Joseph, making him second in command over all Egypt.

The final chapters of Genesis tell how, during the famine, which extended to the land of Canaan, Joseph's brothers went to Egypt to purchase grain, not once but twice. On the second trip, Joseph treated them as spies and demanded that Reuben be kept in custody while they returned to Canaan and came back with Benjamin as proof that they were "honest men" (Genesis 42:19). They did not recognize this Egyptian ruler as the brother they had sold into slavery, yet it is to him that their thoughts turn. While discussing their predicament among themselves, they said, "In truth we are guilty concerning our brother, in that we saw the distress of his soul, when he begged us and we did not listen." And Reuben said, "So now there comes a reckoning for his blood" (Genesis 42:21–22). They did not realize this "Egyptian" ruler understood them because he was using an interpreter.

In the end, after Joseph sees Benjamin alive and reveals himself, the brothers reconcile. Joseph sends

Joseph Forgives His Brothers (Genesis 45), chromolithograph, published in 1886 - Illustration

them home to reveal the truth to their father, Jacob/Israel, and bring him to Egypt, where he lived out his life. Even so after Jacob had died, his older brothers still feared that Joseph would repay them for what they had done to him. Joseph's response is classic:

> "Do not fear, for am I in the place of God? As for you, **you meant evil against me, but God meant it for good,** to bring it about that many people should be kept alive, as they are today. So do not fear; I will provide for you and your little ones." (Genesis 50:19–21, emphasis added)

14 Potiphar's Wife
(Genesis 39)

Joseph had been sold to traders, transported to Egypt, and sold to Potiphar, captain of Pharaoh's bodyguards. He was a vulnerable slave in a foreign land.

He was also a good-looking, well-built young man who had made a powerful impression on Potiphar. And on Potiphar's wife. Potiphar placed so much trust in his Hebrew servant that he put Joseph in charge of his entire household. Potiphar's wife wanted to add to his duties.

She seems to have had little use for subtleties. Her approach consisted of looking Joseph up and down, and then saying, "Lie with me" (Genesis 39:7).

If Joseph was tempted by her offer, he didn't let on. He reminded her of the tremendous responsibilities her husband had given him—of the trust he had placed in Joseph.

He asked, "How then can I do this great wickedness and sin against God?" (Genesis 39:9). Joseph wasn't concerned about being caught by a jealous husband—or about crossing one of the most powerful men in Egypt. For all his loyalty to Potiphar, Joseph was most afraid of offending the God of his forefathers.

Potiphar's wife paid little heed. The next day, she was at it again, insisting that Joseph go to bed with her. Again, Joseph talked his way out of it.

Day after day, she persisted. Day after day, Joseph resisted. And then one day, when all the other servants were out of the house, Potiphar's wife took things a step further. She caught Joseph by his cloak and said, "Lie with me."

Joseph ran. He wriggled free from his cloak and bolted for the door. In his wake, he left a rejected, humiliated, and angry woman. A woman who was holding a piece of his clothing—and looking for revenge.

Potiphar's wife screamed for her servants, telling them:

> "He came in to me to lie with me, and I cried out with a loud voice. And as soon as he heard that I lifted up my voice and cried out, he left his garment beside me and fled and got out of the house." (Genesis 39:14–15)

She told the same story to her husband when he came home. Unfortunately for Joseph, it sounded plausible.

Apparently, the ancient Egyptian legal system wasn't designed to protect the rights of foreign slaves accused of attempting to rape a government official's wife. The investigation, indictment, trial, sentencing, and appeals process seems to have gone like this: Potiphar's wife accused Joseph of trying "to lie" with her; Potiphar apparently believed his wife's story and threw Joseph into the king's prison—where he might have spent the rest of his life. But Genesis 39:21 tells us that "the Lord was with Joseph. . . ."

Joseph and Potiphar's Wife, Guido Reni (1575-1642), c. 1630, oil on canvas.

15 Pharaoh
(Exodus 5–14)

The Israelites were enslaved in Egypt under the pharaoh in the book of Exodus. Pharaoh sanctioned the mistreatment of his enslaved workers in order to maximize their output.

When Moses delivered the message of the Hebrew God to Pharaoh, saying "Let my people go" (5:1), it must have seemed absurd to the Egyptian ruler. He said he did not know the Hebrew God and showed his displeasure by increasing the Hebrew slaves' workload. Instead of supplying them with straw to make bricks, as was the custom, he demanded that the Israelites find the straw themselves—yet still make their brick quota. Pharaoh made the Israelites even more miserable, and he blamed Moses for it.

According to Exodus 7–12, nine plagues struck Egypt in quick succession. The water of the Nile River turned to blood. Frogs invaded the land, followed by enormous swarms of gnats and then flies. Livestock died. An outbreak of painful boils afflicted the Egyptian populace. Extraordinarily large hail killed people and animals and destroyed crops. Swarms of locusts devoured Egypt's vegetation. The sky went pitch-dark for three days. After each disaster, Pharaoh refused to let the Hebrews go.

In the tenth plague, the LORD struck down the first-born in every Egyptian household, including the royal palace. The grief-stricken Pharaoh told Moses to take the Hebrews out of his kingdom.

Pharaoh set out after Moses and the escaping Israelites, pinning them against the shores of the Red Sea, where the LORD had told them to camp so that he could "get glory over Pharaoh and all his host" (14:4). According to Exodus 14, Moses lifted his staff and raised his hand over the sea, and the waters of the sea opened up so that the Hebrews could pass through on dry ground. Pharaoh's army tried to follow, but the waters collapsed on top of them, killing every Egyptian soldier who entered the sea.

Moses and Aaron before Pharaoh. Le Sainte Bible: Traduction nouvelle selon la Vulgate par Mm. J.-J. Bourasse et P. Janvier. Tours: Alfred Mame et Fils. 1866, France, Gustave Doré.

23

16 Pharaoh's Daughter
(Exodus 2)

17 Jochebed
(Exodus 2; Exodus 6:20)

Stained glass window depicts Moses found in a basket in the Nile by Pharaoh's daughter, in the cathedral of Brussels.

Pharaoh's daughter was bathing in the Nile when she noticed a basket floating among the reeds near the bank. She opened it and found a baby inside, and had compassion on him.

Pharaoh had ordered every Hebrew baby boy to be killed. Her motives for adopting the boy and bringing him to live at the royal palace remain unclear. The Bible says only that the child became her son, which likely meant that she gave him access to the finest possessions, the finest education, and the finest opportunities Egypt had to offer.

The biblical narrative offers no insight into her thoughts or feelings when Moses returned years later, claiming to speak for the Hebrew God and demanding the release of the entire Hebrew slave population.

The Rest of the Story

Jewish tradition holds that Pharaoh's daughter was named Bithiah. She was banished from Egypt for bringing Moses into her father's house. When the Israelites began their exodus, Bithiah accompanied them. She later married Mered the Judahite and had three children: Miriam, Shammai, and Ishbah.

Moses's mother, Jochebed, and her people, the Hebrews, were slave laborers. They were also a threat to their Egyptian captors when their numbers increased. To keep the slave population manageable, Pharaoh issued a decree that all Hebrew male babies were to be killed as soon as they were born.

Jochebed already had two children, her son Aaron and his younger sister Miriam. Both were unaffected by Pharaoh's decree. But when she gave birth to her third child—a boy—he was caught in Pharaoh's crosshairs.

This desperate but quick-thinking Hebrew mother fashioned a waterproof basket for her newborn and placed him in the Nile River.

Pharaoh's daughter found the baby and decided to keep him as her own. A nearby Hebrew girl, Moses's sister, asked Pharaoh's daughter if she would like her to find a Hebrew woman to nurse and care for the baby.

Moses's sister brought her Jochebed.

Moses's biological mother was able to maintain a presence and influence in her son's life until the Egyptian royal family adopted him. At that time, Pharaoh's daughter named him Moses "Because," she said, "I drew him out of the water" (Exodus 2:10).

Travel Photography of Rome / Italy: Statue of the daughter of the Pharaoh finding Moses in his basket, at the Pincio at the top of the Piazza del Popolo

18 Jethro
(Exodus 18)

Sometimes even the most powerful leaders need guidance and direction. Moses was overwhelmed by the responsibilities that had fallen on him in the wake of the Hebrews' exodus from Egypt. The Hebrew people were coming to him to settle their legal and personal disputes. From morning till evening, Moses listened to their cases and issued his judgments.

Moses's father-in-law, Jethro, who served as a priest in Midian, observed Moses judging the people from morning till evening. One day, Jethro warned Moses that he was going to burn out. He urged him to establish judges to oversee people groups of thousands, hundreds, fifties, and tens. Those officials would hear the cases that were brought to them and issue their judgments. Only the cases that proved too difficult for them would be brought to Moses.

Thanks to Jethro's strategy for delegating responsibility, Moses was free to focus almost exclusively on his role as the spokesperson for the God of Israel.

19 Aaron
(Exodus 4, 7–8, 32–34; Numbers 16–17)

When God gave Moses the task of delivering the Israelites from Egypt, Moses was reluctant to go. God reunited him with his older brother Aaron to assist him. According to Exodus 4:29–31, Aaron and Moses went to the Hebrew elders and explained God's plan of deliverance.

Aaron stood next to Moses and demanded that Pharaoh release his Hebrew slaves. When God performed signs and plagues to demonstrate his power, Aaron was his instrument on several occasions: his staff became a snake (Exodus 7:10); his staff turned the Nile River to blood (Exodus 7:19); and he used his staff to summon frogs from the waters of Egypt (Exodus 8:6).

In Exodus 17, when the Israelites fought against the Amalekites, an interesting event is mentioned. As long as Moses held his hands up, the Israelites would win, but when they fell, Amalek would win. But he soon got tired, and Aaron was one of the two men who held Moses's hands up during the battle.

In Exodus 28–30, God appointed Aaron and his sons to serve as priests, a role that would be passed down in Aaron's family for generations to come. As a leader, Aaron made his share of mistakes. In Exodus 32, when Moses had been on the mountain with God for so long, the people persuaded Aaron to make a golden calf for them to worship. Later, he, along with his sister Miriam, opposed Moses's leadership (Numbers 12:1–4).

Despite Aaron's indiscretions, the Bible says God still used him along with Moses to guide an unruly group of people through the desert. Later, when the Israelites opposed Aaron's right to the priesthood (Numbers 16–17), God confirmed Aaron as his priest by causing his staff to blossom and produce almonds. When God sent a plague among the people for their rebellion, Aaron was told by Moses to offer incense to spare their lives.

Aaron held the solemn office of priest and left a legacy that extended to the period of the New Testament, where we learn in Luke 1:5 that the parents of John the Baptist, Zechariah and Elizabeth, were descendants of Aaron.

Image changed, new caption needed?

20 Miriam
(Exodus 15; Numbers 12)

Elegant hand-drawn isolated traditional Jewish sacred amulet and religious symbols - Hamsa or hand of Miriam, palm of David, star of David, Rosh Hashanah, Hanukkah, Shana Tova.

Miriam spoke for the God of Israel. She delivered prophecies in his name. Many scholars believe that the song sung by Miriam in Exodus 15 is one of the oldest texts in the Hebrew Bible, and is thought by many scholars to be the earlier of the two songs in that chapter.

Yet she was—and is—forever known as the sister of Moses.

Miriam served alongside of one of Israel's most beloved prophets and leaders. The fact that they shared the same parents must have added layers of complexity to their working relationship.

Miriam's brothers, Moses, and Aaron, overshadowed her in the text. She led her people in worship after Moses led them through the parted waters of the Red Sea. Miriam led the women in singing a refrain of the song Moses sings in Exodus 15 about the people's escape from Egypt:

Then Miriam the prophetess, the sister of Aaron, took a tambourine in her hand, and all the women went out after her with tambourines and dancing. And Miriam sang to them:
  "Sing to the Lord, for he has triumphed gloriously;
  the horse and his rider he has thrown into the sea."

But she couldn't compete with Moses, who spoke face-to-face with the God of their people.

The Bible records that Miriam and Aaron's frustration came to a boil over Moses's marriage to a Cushite woman. Miriam and Aaron lost their composure and challenged Moses's leadership.

According to Numbers 12, the LORD was displeased by Aaron and Miriam's outburst. For challenging Moses, Miriam was struck with a disease that turned her skin white. Moses interceded on her behalf after Aaron's apology, and eventually God healed her.

Miriam's record of service and leadership cannot be negated by one ill-considered outburst. She holds an esteemed place in Israel's history.

Moses in the Bulrushes, Paul Delaroche (1797-1856), c. 1857.

21 Moses
(Exodus 1–40)

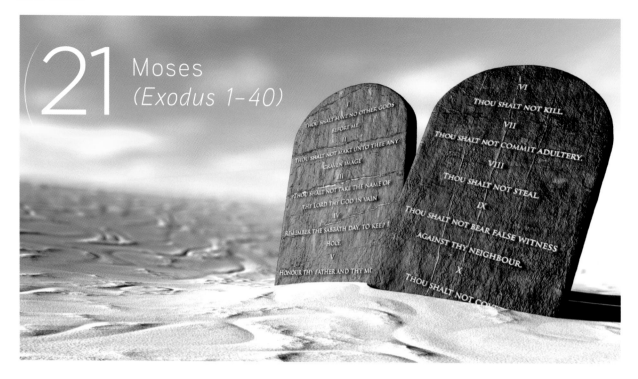

Moses's extraordinary life began with a brush with death. Born to Hebrew slaves in Egypt, Moses escaped Pharaoh's execution order for all Hebrew male babies through the quick thinking of his mother, Jochebed . She placed him in a watertight basket and set him in the Nile River. The princess of Egypt, Pharaoh's daughter, found him and adopted him as her own.

Moses's future in Egypt came to an end when he saw an Egyptian overseer beating a Hebrew slave. Moses stepped in to protect the slave and killed the Egyptian.

With Egyptian blood on his hands, Moses fled to the wilderness and started a new life tending flocks. His life on the run was interrupted by an extraordinary encounter. According to Exodus 3, the God of the Hebrews (written with the consonants YHWH) spoke to him from a bush that was on fire but did not burn. He instructed Moses to return to Egypt and demand that Pharaoh release the Hebrew slaves.

Moses risked his life to confront Pharaoh. The Egyptian ruler let the Israelites go only after ten plagues devastated his kingdom. Moses led multitudes of Hebrew slaves out of Egypt toward a land that the LORD had promised them.

They arrived at the shores of the Red Sea, only to learn that God had hardened Pharaoh's heart and changed his mind, and that he and his army were bearing down on them at that very moment. The newly freed slaves panicked; Moses did not. LORD told him to lift his staff and stretch out his hand over the sea, "and the LORD drove the sea back by a strong east wind all night and made the sea dry land, and the waters were divided. And the people of Israel went into the midst of the sea on dry ground, the waters being a wall to them on their right hand and on their left" (Exodus 14:21–22). When the Egyptians tried to follow, the waters closed, killing them all.

Moses led the Hebrews through the wilderness. Exodus 19–20 records that at Mount Sinai, he climbed to the summit alone to receive the Law from God himself.

The Hebrews proved to be a difficult people to lead. They complained bitterly about life in the wilderness. According to the Exodus narrative, God provided them with manna to eat and sent water flowing from rocks to quench their thirst. At times they still longed for their old lives as slaves in Egypt.

Moses kept a relatively cool head through it all—with one exception. Numbers 20 records an account in which God instructed Moses to speak to a rock so that water would pour from it. Instead, Moses struck the rock.

For his disobedience, Moses was forbidden to enter the land of Canaan, though the LORD allowed him to see it from a high mountain. Still, he led the Israelites to the very edge of their destination.

22 Joshua
(Joshua 1–24)

Joshua was one of twelve spies Moses sent to scout the land of Canaan. Ten of the spies returned with bad news. They warned Moses and the Hebrew people that the people in Canaan were strong, large, and lived in fortified cities.

Caleb presented the minority opinion. Joshua and Caleb then urged the Hebrews to attack immediately. They reasoned that if they had the LORD on their side, they would be victorious.

Joshua and Caleb were overruled, and the Hebrews refused to fight for the land. As punishment, God sentenced the Hebrews to wander in the wilderness for forty years, until the faithless generation had died.

Forty years later, Joshua assumed leadership from Moses, who had been forbidden by God from entering Canaan, and had died. With great ceremony and purposefulness, Joshua led the Israelites across the Jordan River into the land God had promised their ancestors. The Hebrew people finally were ready to fight for what was promised them. First stop: the walled city of Jericho.

According to Joshua 6:2, the LORD himself delivered battle instructions to Joshua. Once a day for six days, the Hebrews were to march around the city in complete silence. On the seventh day, they were to march around it seven times. The seventh time around, seven priests were to blow trumpets and all the people were to shout.

Joshua followed the instructions completely. The trumpets sounded, the people shouted, the walls of Jericho collapsed, and the Hebrews laid waste to the city. It was the first of many victories for Joshua.

Joshua later oversaw the distribution of land to the various tribes of Israel. In his old age, he—and all of Israel—enjoyed a season of peace.

Ancient ruins of one of the oldest human cities, Jericho.

23 Caleb
(Numbers 13–14; Joshua 14–15)

Caleb is a hero for the sidekicks, the behind-the-scenes folks, and the honorable mentions.

Moses sent twelve spies into Canaan to scout the land and assess the inhabitants. Ten of them returned with pessimistic reports of giants in the land and warnings against trying to invade. But two of them returned full of optimism, confident that the God of Israel would give them victory, regardless of their opponents' strength and size.

One of those faithful spies was Joshua, who was chosen by God to succeed Moses. Joshua led the Hebrew people across the Jordan River into Canaan. He led the attacks against the strongholds in the land. He drove out the Canaanites so that the Hebrews could settle the land that was promised to their ancestors.

The other faithful spy was Caleb. In the narrative found in the book of Numbers, Caleb is every bit as faithful and courageous as Joshua. Yet not much is heard of Caleb after his espionage adventure. He led the attack on Hebron, the place of the giants (the Nephilim), and asked for the most difficult land as an inheritance.

In his lifetime, Caleb never received the fame or lofty position that Joshua experienced, but he will forever be known as one of the only two men who had enough confidence to fight for the land God had promised. God said of him, "But my servant Caleb, because he has a different spirit and has followed me fully, I will bring into the land into which he went, and his descendants shall possess it" (Numbers 14:24). He and Joshua were the only men of their generation to survive the wilderness wanderings and enter the land of Canaan.

Joshua and Caleb, coloured engraving by Cornelis Vissher, Netherlands, 17th century

24 Rahab
(Joshua 2)

Characters of ill-repute who stand by the hero after all of the "decent" folk have deserted him is a familiar trope.

In the Old Testament, Rahab of Jericho fills that role. She had everything to lose by helping the two Hebrew spies who hid at her house. Yet when the soldiers of Jericho came to arrest the spies, the Hebrews were nowhere to be found. Rahab had hidden them under stalks of flax on her roof.

Rahab conceals the spies. Illustration to book of Joshua, 2. 3 -6 : 'The King of Jericho sent unto Rahab, saying, Bring forth the men that are come to thee, which are entered into thine house; for they be come to search out all the country. But she brought them up to the roof of the house, and hid them with the stalks of flax'. Chromolithograph plate by Kronheim.

Top Four

The Midrash—the ancient texts that offer commentary on the Torah—lists Rahab as one of the four most beautiful women who ever lived. Sarah, Abigail, and Esther round out the quartet.

"I know that the LORD has given you the land," she told the spies. "Now then, please swear to me by the LORD that, as I have dealt kindly with you, you also will deal kindly with my father's house, and give me a sure sign that you will save alive my father and mother, my brothers and sisters, and all who belong to them, and deliver our lives from death" (Joshua 2:9, 12–13).

Rahab's scheme paid off. The spies told Rahab to tie a scarlet cord in her window—and then the spies escaped by following Rahab's instructions. The Israelites' attack on Jericho commenced shortly thereafter. The invaders decimated the city and killed its inhabitants—with a few notable exceptions.

Everyone in the house with the scarlet cord in the window was spared. Rahab saved her entire family by risking her life to hide the Hebrew spies.

Rahab lived out the remainder of her days among the Israelites. But her story doesn't end there. The New Testament book of James refers to her courageous deed. She is listed with Abraham, Moses, and David in the "Faith Hall of Fame" in Hebrews 11.

Perhaps most importantly, she is found in the genealogy in Matthew 1. Rahab and Salmon are listed as the parents of Boaz—and the direct ancestors of David and Jesus.

25 Og
(Numbers 21; Deuteronomy 3)

26 Balaam
(Numbers 22–24)

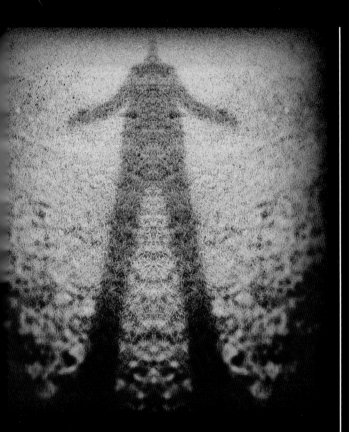

Balaam is at the center of one of the strangest stories in the Old Testament. He was an outsider (he hailed from Pethor) who was brought to Moab to curse the Israelites. The narrative in the book of Numbers suggests that he was a prophet or a soothsayer.

Balak, the king of the Moabites, sent princes from his kingdom with gifts to recruit Balaam for a special assignment. The Moabites were at war with Israel, and Balak wanted Balaam to pronounce a curse on the Israelites.

The God of Israel came and spoke to Balaam, and would not allow him to leave with Balak's representatives.

Balaam blessing Israel despite Balak, King of Moab's attempts to use this enchanter and seer to curse the Israelites.

All the Hebrews wanted was passage through the land of the Amorites on their way to Canaan. Among others, standing in their way was Og, the king of Bashan. The Old Testament narrative suggests that he was a formidable obstacle. According to Deuteronomy 3:11, Og was the last of the Rephaim, a race of giants. (The verse describes his bed as being nine cubits long and four cubits wide—that is, approximately 13.5 feet by 6 feet.)

Og and his armies attacked the Hebrews at Edrei. According to the biblical texts, the outcome of the battle was never in question. The LORD assured Moses that he would deliver Og, along with his people and land, into the Israelites' hands. When the fighting stopped, Og and his people were dead, his cities were destroyed, and Bashan's livestock and possessions were Hebrew plunder.

Balaam and the Ass, James J. Tissot 1836-1902/French Jewish Museum, New York.

So Balak sent more prestigious representatives and authorized them to offer Balaam more valuable gifts. The God of Israel comes to Balaam again, and this time gives him permission to go with the messengers, warning him, "but only do what I tell you" (Numbers 22:20).

Balaam mounted his donkey and rode away with the Moabites, but his trip was far more adventurous and dangerous than he expected. Three times his donkey stopped dead in its tracks. Three times Balaam struck his donkey to coax it to move. Numbers 22:28-30 continues the story:

> Then the Lord opened the mouth of the donkey, and she said to Balaam, "What have I done to you, that you have struck me these three times?" And Balaam said to the donkey, "Because you have made a fool of me. I wish I had a sword in my hand, for then I would kill you." And the donkey said to Balaam, "Am I not your donkey, on which you have ridden all your life long to this day? Is it my habit to treat you this way?" And he said, "No."

Balaam looked up and saw what the donkey had seen: an angel with a sword, ready to kill him. Balaam fell on his face before the angel and confessed his sin. The angel allowed him to continue on with the Moabites, warning him again, "Go with the men, but speak only the word that I tell you" (Numbers 22:35).

In Moab, Balak took Balaam to several high vantage points where he could see the Israelite forces spread out below him. Four times Balak urged Balaam to pronounce a curse on the Israelites. Four times Balaam was able to utter only the words the Lord put in his mouth. Instead of cursing the Israelites, he blessed them.

Numbers 25 and 31 record his attempt to sabotage the Israelites another way, when he advised the Midianites to entice the Israelites into worshiping their

a plague on the people of Israel in which 24,000 people were killed.

The New Testament refers to Balaam's negative character in 2 Peter 2:15 and Jude 11. Revelation 2:14 sums it up this way:

> "But I have a few things against you: you have some there who hold the teaching of Balaam, who taught Balak to put a stumbling block before the sons of Israel, so that they might eat food sacrificed to idols and practice sexual immorality."

27 Achan
(Joshua 7)

The instructions were very clear: *Do not take any spoils from Jericho.* The fall of the well-known walled city marked the beginning of the Hebrews' conquest of Canaan. Everyone and everything within its walls were to be destroyed. Nothing was to be taken as plunder.

With their rousing victory fresh in their minds, the Israelites marched on to the small town of Ai. But the forces of Ai dealt a devastating defeat to the Hebrews. Joshua, their shell-shocked leader, consulted God to find out what happened. God revealed to Joshua that someone within the Hebrew camp had violated his command and taken forbidden spoils from Jericho. The Hebrew leaders cast lots to discover who had disobeyed.

A man named Achan was revealed to be the culprit. Because of his actions, the anger of God burned against the entire nation. Achan's punishment was swift and severe. He and his entire family, along with the animals in their household, were stoned and burned to death, along with all of their possessions and ill-gotten gains from Jericho.

Casting Lots

The casting of lots was a common practice in the Old Testament, used by various people to make important decisions.

The method used to cast lots is not stated in the Bible. According to Proverbs 16:33, it was the Lord who directed the outcome; thus, the lots determined the will of God.

Achan and his Family Stoned to Death, James J. Tissot 1836-1902/ French Jewish Museum New York.

(28 Deborah
(Judges 4)

In the book of Judges, the Israelites faced severe oppression from Jabin, the king of Canaan. Jabin's top military man was a commander named Sisera, whose fighting force included 900 iron chariots. Sisera and his Canaanite army dominated the Israelites for twenty long years.

The Israelites needed a leader who would be brave enough to challenge Jabin and Sisera—and also inspiring enough to rally the Israelite forces to battle.

Her name was Deborah.

She was known as a prophetess and judge who plied her trade from beneath a palm tree in the hill country of Ephraim. According to Judges 4, the people of Israel came to her to settle their disputes. They looked to her for guidance and wisdom.

In response to the mounting Canaanite problem, Deborah instructed Barak, the military leader of the Benjamites, to raise an army of 10,000 Israelites. The LORD would deliver the Canaanites into their hands, she told him.

Barak's response speaks volumes about the esteem in which Deborah was held: "If you will not go with me, I will not go."

Deborah promised to go, but told him a woman would be the one to kill Sisera: "I will surely go with you," she replied. "Nevertheless, the road on which you are going will not lead to your glory, for the LORD will sell Sisera into the hand of a woman." (See the story of Jael for the fulfillment of Deborah's prophecy.)

Barak led the Israelites to victory over the Canaanites.

Deborah the judge

35

29 Jael
(Judges 4-5)

Jael recognized the intruder in her tent immediately. Sisera, the ruthless Canaanite commander who had terrorized Israel for twenty years, was on the run. His forces had been decimated in battle; he was the lone survivor. And now the Israelite army was after him. A tent among a family that was at peace with Sisera's king must have seemed like a safe hiding place to him.

Jael wasn't an Israelite, but her people, the Kenites, lived nearby and allied themselves with the Israelites.

Sisera asked for hospitality, and Jael obliged him. She attended to the Canaanite military leader's needs until he went to sleep.

Perhaps the furthest thing from the commander's mind as he drifted off to sleep was the notion that Jael—a woman whose house was at peace with his people might try to harm him. The nearest thing to his mind, though, was the sharpened tent peg that Jael hammered through his skull.

Jael kept a cool head and a steady hand. She seized the opportunity that presented itself and accomplished what the Israelite forces had been trying to do for two decades. With one act, Jael put the fearsome commander Sisera out of Israel's misery.

Barak and Deborah, the Israelite prophetess and judge who accompanied the forces that sent Sisera running in the first place, celebrated Jael in song. In their words, we find the epitaph for the woman who put an end to one of Israel's oppressors:

"Most blessed of women be Jael."

Jael and Sisera
Picture from The Holy Scriptures, Old and New Testaments book collection published in 1885, Stuttgart Germany. Drawings by Gustave Dore.

(30 Gideon
(Judges 6)

Gideon's triumph over the Midianites is an incredible story!

According to the book of Judges, an angel of the LORD appeared to Gideon when he was beating out grain in a wine press. At the time, Gideon was hiding from the Midianites, the desert marauders who stole the Israelites' food, destroyed their livestock, and laid waste to their land.

"The LORD is with you, O mighty man of valor," the angel said (Judges 6:12).

Mighty man of valor was not how Gideon saw himself. When the angel informed him that the God of Israel had chosen him to deliver Israel from the Midianites, Gideon's response was disbelief. "Please, Lord, how can I save Israel? Behold, my clan is the weakest in Manasseh, and I am the least in my father's house" (Judges 6:15).

Gideon asked God to confirm his calling with an unmistakable sign. He left a fleece on the ground overnight and asked God to make the dew settle only on the fleece, leaving the ground around it dry. The next morning, the fleece was soaked and the ground was dry.

Still not quite convinced, Gideon left the fleece out overnight again. This time, he asked God to leave the fleece dry. The next morning, the ground was soaked and the fleece was dry.

That was all Gideon needed to see. He assembled an army of 32,000 men to battle the Midianites. The LORD told him he had too many. He instructed Gideon to reduce his forces by releasing anyone who was fearful about the coming battle. Twenty-two thousand men deserted. That left Gideon a fighting force of 10,000 to battle a foe that Judges 7:12 describes as "like locusts in abundance."

The LORD still didn't like the numbers. He ordered Gideon to pare down his army even more, based on the way his men drank water from a stream. When the paring was done, Gideon was left with only 300 men. Those were the men he took into battle.

He divided them into three companies and gave each soldier a trumpet and a pitcher with a torch in it. His army sneaked into the Midianite camp under cover of darkness. At Gideon's signal, they blew their trumpets and smashed their pitchers.

In the resulting confusion, the LORD caused the Midianites to attack one another and flee. Gideon and his men didn't let them escape. The small group of 300 warriors killed and pursued the Midianites.

After the battle, the Israelites appealed to Gideon to rule over them. Even in victory, the man knew his place. "I will not rule over you, and my son will not rule over you; the LORD will rule over you" (Judges 8:23).

A sheep being shorn with hand clippers. The wool that is removed will become a fleece similar to the one that is referred to in Gideon's story.

(31) Samson
Judges 13–16

In the story of Samson and Delilah, readers are introduced to a hero who slaughtered more than 1,000 Philistine men yet pursued risky romances with Philistine women . . . a hero who set fire to 300 foxes to burn the crops of his enemies . . . a hero set apart to God from birth, yet who often broke with Jewish law.

The time of the judges had been a difficult transitional period in Israel's history. The people had been united under Moses, and then under Joshua's leadership they had cleared out most of the Canaanite strongholds. But after Joshua sent the tribes to fend for themselves in their previously assigned territories, worship became decentralized, skirmishes continued with the Canaanites, and the newly independent tribes often failed to resolve the challenges they were facing. The next generation of people was already worshiping the gods of Canaan (Judges 2:10–15), provoking the LORD to anger.

The book of Judges details the destructive cycle that had repeated itself throughout this era:

❋ The Israelites would rebel against their God's commandments—usually by engaging in idolatry.

❋ As punishment, God would allow their enemies to oppress and defeat them.

❋ Eventually the chastened and demoralized Israelites would call out to God for help.

❋ God would send a judge—a political and/ or military leader—to deliver them from their enemies.

Samson was the final judge sent to Israel during this period. His origin story reads like something from a graphic novel. An angel told Samson's mother that her unborn son would be set apart for the LORD's service and bound by strict vows. He was forbidden to drink wine (or eat anything made with grapes), not become ritually impure from corpses or graves (that is, not come in contact with them), and not cut his hair, which displayed his special dedication to the vow. In return, the LORD would bless his efforts to lead the Israelites against the Philistines.

As it turned out, the LORD had endowed Samson with superhuman strength. He singlehandedly killed 1,000 Philistines using the jawbone of a donkey. He tied together the tails of 300 foxes, put torches between them, and released them into the Philistines' grain fields, vineyards, and olive groves. Later, when the Philistines tried to trap him, he pulled up the city gates and walked off with them on his shoulders—doors, posts, bar, and all.

Yet Samson was repeatedly drawn to Philistine women. He arranged to marry one but was tricked at the wedding party by her friends and family. Later, he fell for a woman named Delilah. Samson's enemies persuaded Delilah to betray Samson in exchange for financial reward. She convinced Samson to reveal the secret of his strength.

While he slept on Delilah's lap, the Philistines cut his hair. When he awoke, his strength was gone. The

32 Delilah
(Judges 16)

Philistines seized him, gouged out his eyes, and forced him to grind grain in prison.

From the depths of captivity, however, Samson took one final stand. As the Philistines celebrated his capture with a feast honoring their god Dagon, thousands gathered in the temple to eat, drink, and gloat. Samson was paraded before them and then left between two great stone pillars in their temple.

Samson was blind and bound, but he was no longer helpless. The Philistines failed to notice that his hair had grown back.

Samson prayed to the LORD to give him strength one last time. He placed his hands on the pillars that supported the temple and pushed. As the roof collapsed on top of them, thousands of Philistines were brought to their death. Samson sacrificed his own life to avenge himself for the loss of his eyes.

Samson and Delilah. Artist: Cranach, Lucas, the Younger (1515-1586)

The rulers of Philistia were desperate. Samson, the extraordinarily powerful Israelite, had wreaked havoc on their nation for years. The man set fire to their fields and orchards. He killed one thousand of their soldiers in a single battle—by himself. He tore out the gates of Gaza, one of their capital cities, with his bare hands.

Over a period of twenty years, Samson's victories demoralized the Philistines. None of their strategies to subdue him seemed to work. The man was nearly invincible.

Nearly.

The Philistine rulers finally discovered a kink in their enemy's proverbial armor that they could exploit: Samson's fondness for women. When he fell in love with a woman named Delilah, the lords of the Philistines bribed her with a promise of 1,100 pieces of silver a piece if she succeeded.

Delilah seduced him and began to ask Samson about his secret, "Please tell me what makes you so strong and what it would take to tie you up securely." The love-struck strongman told her that if he were tied up with seven new bowstrings, he would become as weak as anyone else.

Shortly thereafter, he fell asleep on Delilah's lap. Delilah and her co-conspirators tied him up with seven new bowstrings. But when Philistine troops came to get him, he broke the strings like thread.

Delilah upbraided Samson for lying to her. Twice more she asked him the secret of his strength. Twice more he gave her false replies. Twice more a group of Philistines came to seize him, only to be scared away by a still-strong Samson.

After three such incidents, many men might have become quite suspicious. Yet day after day, Delilah continued to prod Samson to reveal the secret of his strength. Worn out by her constant cajoling, Samson finally revealed that if his hair were cut, he would become as weak as any other man.

Satisfied, Delilah encouraged Samson to sleep. While he lay with his head on her lap, she called for someone to

The Manipulation

"And she said to him, 'How can you say, "I love you," when your heart is not with me? You have mocked me these three times, and you have not told me where your great strength lies.' And when she pressed him hard with her words day after day, and urged him, his soul was vexed to death." (Judges 16:15-16)

cut his hair. This time when the Philistines came for him, Samson found he had no strength to resist them.

Delilah's role in the story ends there—but the questions don't. Did the Israelite strongman give Delilah one last look before his enemies blinded him and took him to prison? Did he see the thousands of silver coins she was paid to betray him?

Was Delilah present at the festival to honor the Philistine god Dagon? Did she weep at the sight of the blind and seemingly helpless Samson being taunted by the crowd? Did she notice that his hair had grown back before he placed his hands on the load-bearing pillars of the temple?

Regardless of whether Delilah might have been among the 3,000 Philistines on the roof or those packed into the temple beneath, she was an unwitting accomplice to what happened next. Because of her betrayal, Samson found himself in a position to do more damage than ever before. The Bible says that Samson's death toll the day he collapsed the temple greatly exceeded the number of Philistines he had killed during his twenty-year tenure as Israel's judge (Judges 16:30-31).

Fresco of Delilah, woman of Samson from 19th century in Altlerchenfelder church, Vienna.

33 Ruth
(Ruth 1)

Boaz and Ruth in the book of Ruth. Boaz allows Ruth to glean from his fields during the harvesting because he has heard of her kidnness to her mother-in-law, Naomi. Illustration by William Hole 1846 - 1917

How can a humble, foreign woman play a part in the history of Israel?

Widows were especially vulnerable in the ancient world. The loss of a husband meant the loss of security and well-being. Widows had to depend on others—usually their children or other family members—to provide for them. In every possible way, widows were often at the mercy of others.

The book of Ruth opens with an especially tragic tale of widowhood. A woman named Naomi and her two daughters-in-law, Orpah and Ruth, all lose their husbands in quick succession. For Naomi, the loss was especially acute. She suddenly had no husband and no sons to provide for her.

Naomi was an Israelite woman living alone in Moab. With no other option, she decided to return to her homeland of Judah to live out her final years. Orpah and Ruth, who were both Moabites, dutifully agreed to accompany her. Naomi realized that her homeland held no promise for them, so she released them from their responsibility to her and urged them to remain in Moab with their own people.

Orpah and Ruth considered their options carefully. Orpah accepted the release Naomi offered and chose to stay in Moab. Perhaps she hoped to find a new husband there from among her own people.

Out of loyalty, Ruth set aside her own hopes for the future in order to care for Naomi. She accompanied her mother-in-law to Judah.

Once in Judah, the two women struggled to survive. Ruth foraged for food left behind by harvesters in the field. Things looked bleak until they met Boaz, a wealthy relative of Naomi's late husband. In keeping with ancient tradition, Boaz agreed to buy land that belonged to Naomi. As part of the transaction, he also agreed to marry Ruth and continue Naomi's family line in accordance with the Law of Moses.

Ruth, the ever-faithful daughter-in-law, secured a measure of happiness and peace for Naomi and herself in the wake of their loss.

34 Hannah
(1 Samuel 1)

I n an ancient culture that prized fertility, a barren woman was an object of shame and speculation. Infertility was blamed on a woman's spiritual failing—perceived to be a symbol of God's displeasure.

Hannah was barren. To make matters worse, she shared her home—and her husband, Elkanah—with a second wife, Peninnah. First Samuel 1:2 describes the situation this way: "Peninnah had children, but Hannah did not."

Peninnah taunted Hannah about her childless condition. Elkanah offered comfort to his beloved wife. "Hannah, why do you weep? And why do you not eat? And why is your heart sad? Am I not more to you than ten sons?"

The Bible doesn't record Hannah's reply.

Hannah took her pain and suffering to the temple of the LORD in Shiloh. She wept. She prayed. She made a vow to give her firstborn son to God for a lifetime of service, if only God would allow her to get pregnant. When her voice faltered, she silently mouthed her prayer.

Eli, the priest, misinterpreted the scene. "How long will you go on being drunk?" he asked. "Put your wine away from you."

Hannah was not dissuaded. She pleaded her case to the priest, who was moved by her anguish and sorrow. "Go in peace," Eli said, "and the God of Israel grant your petition that you have made to him."

The Bible tells us that "in due time" Hannah conceived and bore a son.

Nine months later, she gave birth to Samuel. She weaned her son and then fulfilled her vow. Hannah took Samuel back to Shiloh and left him there with Eli. In 1 Samuel 2, Hannah expresses her pride, joy, relief, vindication, and thankfulness in song.

Hannah presenting her son Samuel to the priest Eli, Stained glass window in Basilica of St. Vitus in Ellwangen, Germany.

(35 Samuel
(1 Samuel 1–12)

The young boy, Samuel, made his home in the temple at Shiloh because, before he was born, his mother had committed him to a life of religious service. As he lay down to sleep one night, he heard a voice call to him. He ran to the room of Eli, the high priest. "Here I am," the boy said, "for you called me" (1 Samuel 3:4).

"I did not call," Eli informed him. "Lie down again" (1 Samuel 3:5).

The voice called a second time. The boy ran to Eli's room again, only to be told again that Eli hadn't called him.

The boy lay down again. The voice called a third time. This time when the boy went to Eli's room, the high priest realized what was happening—and where the voice was coming from. He gave the boy specific instructions on how to respond.

Samuel lay down again. The voice called as before, "Samuel! Samuel!" (1 Samuel 3:10).

Samuel responded as Eli had instructed: "Speak, for your servant hears."

In the decades that followed, Samuel served the LORD as a priest, a prophet, and a judge. He emerged as a revered figure in Israel. When Saul was chosen to rule as the nation's king, it was Samuel who anointed him. When the time came to choose Saul's successor, it was Samuel who approached the youngest son of Jesse, a young man named David.

In the earliest days of Israel's monarchy, the prophet Samuel led Israel into repentance from idolatry and recommitment to the LORD. When he died, the entire nation mourned for him.

The prophet Samuel by Claude Vignon, 1593-1670, France.

36 Saul
(1 Samuel 9–31)

He should have been a hero.

He looked the part. According to 1 Samuel 9:2, he was a handsome man who stood head and shoulders above his fellow Israelites.

He had the credentials. The LORD chose him to serve as his people's first monarch. This man, Saul, in all his perceived glory, was the answer to the Israelites' prayers.

Saul started strong as king. He led 330,000 soldiers to victory against the Ammonites and saved the city of Jabesh Gilead. Unfortunately, things soon went downhill.

Saul was a great king who protected his people but struggled with insecurity and jealousy.

Saul chose David to serve as his court musician, to play his harp when Saul was troubled by a harmful spirit from the LORD. He gave David his daughter's hand in marriage. Yet, he suspected that David had designs on his throne, even though David showed nothing but loyalty to the king. More than once, Saul's jealousy and the harmful spirit from the LORD drove him to attempt to murder David.

He saw David as his enemy. Marching home from his army's victory over the Philistines—and David's victory over Goliath—Saul was disturbed by the greeting of well-wishers who sang, "Saul has killed his thousands, but David his ten thousands."

In addition to his jealousy of David, Saul had a problem with authority. In 1 Samuel 15, Saul disobeys Samuel's order to attack Amalek and devote everything to destruction, including animals and children. Instead, Saul let the Amalekite king live and spared the best of the animals. Samuel told Saul, "Because you have rejected the word of the Lord, he has also rejected you from being king" (1 Samuel 15:23)

After Samuel died and as darkness began to close in around him, Saul grew desperate. He visited the medium of En-dor, a practitioner of dark arts, and asked her to bring forth the ghost of Samuel. Samuel appeared to Saul and told him that his kingdom had been taken from him, that his army would fall to the Philistines the next day, and that he and his sons would not live to see the end of the battle.

Saul's sons died in battle the next day. Saul himself was gravely wounded by Philistine archers. Rather than allowing the Philistines to kill him and mistreat his body, Saul threw himself on his sword and died.

Saul anointed by Samuel

37 David
(1 Samuel 16–31; 2 Samuel 1–24)

David is known as the beloved king of Israel, and his list of heroic deeds and acts of faithful service is long and impressive.

As a young shepherd, he stepped onto a battlefield, armed with only a sling and a few rocks, to face a heavily armored Philistine giant. He became a national hero—and an enemy of King Saul—when he felled Goliath with a single shot.

David then led several successful military campaigns against the Philistines. When King Saul demanded that David bring him the foreskins (you read that right) of one hundred Philistines in exchange for the privilege of marrying his daughter, David brought him two hundred.

When Saul made attempts on his life, David was forced to flee. During his time on the run, he became an even more cunning warrior and leader. Though he had more than one opportunity to harm Saul during that time, he refused to raise his hand against the man he considered to be "the LORD's anointed."

After Saul's death, David became king. He united the twelve tribes of Israel and arranged to have the ark of the covenant returned to Jerusalem. He honored the vows he made to Israel's allies and settled scores with its enemies. In 1 Chronicles, it says he gathered supplies for the construction of a temple in Jerusalem.

But there are stains on David's record of heroism, one of which is recorded in 2 Samuel 11. He had an affair with Bathsheba, the wife of one of his soldiers, Uriah. When Bathsheba became pregnant, David sent for Uriah from the battlefield. He hoped Uriah would have sex with his wife and everyone would assume that Uriah was the father. When that plan didn't work, David arranged for Uriah to be abandoned during battle and killed by Israel's enemies.

This could have been the end of David's story, but when the prophet Nathan confronted him, David confessed his sin and asked the LORD for forgiveness. Though the child he had conceived with Bathsheba died, God did later bless their union by giving them more children, including David's successor, their son, Solomon (2 Samuel 12:24; 1 Chronicles 3:5).

Almost half the psalms in the Bible are attributed to David, and they reveal both repentance and devotion to God. David's legacy ricochets throughout the Bible.

David and Goliath fresco on medieval house wall, Regensburg, Bavaria, Germany.

38 Michal
(1 Samuel 19)

Michal had watched her father—Saul, the king of Israel—marry off her older sister, Merab. Saul had pledged Merab's hand in marriage to the handsome warrior David—and then changed his mind and married her off to someone else instead. Merab's loss was Michal's gain. Michal was in love with David.

Saul allowed David and Michal to marry, but only because he wanted to keep David close so that the Philistines might kill him instead of having to do it himself. Shortly thereafter, Saul sent some men to make his daughter a widow. Michal helped David escape and then convinced his would-be assassins that her husband was sick in bed. She risked her own life to save David's.

Michal was later married off to a man named Palti (1 Samuel 25). She lived with him for years while David was on the run. David stopped running when Saul died and succeeded Saul as king of Israel.

King David demanded that his wife be returned to him. Unfortunately, their reunion proved to be anticlimactic; their romance was over. That much is evident from their final interaction.

The return of the ark of the covenant to Jerusalem was a time of joyous celebration. David himself led the festivities, dancing with wild abandon. 2 Samuel 6:16 and 20 describe what happened next: "As the ark of the LORD came into the city of David, Michal the daughter of Saul looked out of the window and saw King David leaping and dancing before the LORD, and she despised him in her heart. . . . [She] came out to meet David and said, 'How the king of Israel honored himself today, uncovering himself today before the eyes of his servants' female servants, as one of the vulgar fellows shamelessly uncovers himself!'"

David replied that he would gladly become even more undignified in his worship, if the spirit so moved him. Thus ends the story of David and Michal.

A postscript in 2 Samuel 6:23 notes that Michal remained childless for the rest of her life.

David makes his escape, by J. James Tissot. Illustration to book of Samuel (I), 19.12: 'So Michal let David down through a window: and he went, and fled, and escaped'. Following Saul 's attempt to kill him, David escapes with the help of his wife Michal. JJT: French painter, 15 October 1836 – 8 August 1902.

39 Goliath
(1 Samuel 17)

G oliath was a villain straight out of central casting: enormous, profane, and spoiling for a fight—a bully for the ages. This champion of the Philistines gave the appearance of being an unconquerable foe. Goliath was a mountain of a man, much larger than any soldier in Israel's ranks. He seemed to be more skilled as a warrior and much more heavily armored than anyone in the Israelite army.

The portrait painted in 1 Samuel 17 is one of a blood-thirsty combatant, eager to fight. Goliath did everything he could to provoke the Israelites into sending a champion to meet him in battle. He reminded them of the stakes: if he defeated Israel's champion, then the Israelites would become servants of the Philistines; if the Israelite champion defeated Goliath, then the Philistines would become servants of the Israelites. Twice a day for forty days, the giant Goliath called across the battlefield, taunting the Israelites with supreme confidence.

When a challenger finally emerged from Israel's side, Goliath became enraged. The Israelite competitor was a mere boy, an armorless, swordless civilian carrying nothing but a staff, a sling, and some stones.

"Am I a dog, that you come to me with sticks?" Goliath roared as the boy placed a stone in his sling. "Come to me, and I will give your flesh to the birds of the air and to the beasts of the field" (1 Samuel 17:43–44).

Those were the villain's last recorded words before he was killed by David.

40 Jonathan
(1 Samuel 18-20)

E veryone should have a friend like Jonathan. By tradition, as the oldest son of King Saul, Jonathan stood to inherit his father's throne. Yet, according to the narrative of 1 Samuel, the LORD had already chosen another successor: David, the youngest son of Jesse and the slayer of Goliath.

Rather than vie with David for the crown, Jonathan did everything he could to help, support, and protect David. First Samuel 18:1–5 suggests that the two young men became lifelong friends the first time they met.

Jonathan knew how much his father hated David. So Jonathan stepped in to warn David of his father's plots to kill him. He intervened on David's behalf with his father. He risked Saul's wrath—risked his own life, in fact—to keep his friend David from harm.

Jonathan and his brothers were killed in battle shortly before his father, Saul, committed suicide. David honored his fallen friend by taking care of Jonathan's son, Mephibosheth, for the rest of his life.

David and Jonathan, c.1508. Artist: Cima da Conegliano, Giovanni Battista (ca. 1459-1517)

41 Abigail
(1 Samuel 25)

On paper, it was a mismatch of, well, biblical proportions. According to 1 Samuel, Abigail was "discerning and beautiful." (The Talmud tells us that she was "one of four women of surpassing beauty in the world.") Yet Abigail's physical attributes seem to have been equally matched by her intelligence, diplomacy, and crisis-management skills.

Her husband, Nabal, was far less impressive. His name, in Hebrew, means "fool." The author of 1 Samuel describes the man as "harsh and badly behaved."

To understand why, one need look no further than 1 Samuel 25. David and his band of 600 warriors were on the run from King Saul near Carmel, the hometown of Nabal and Abigail. David and his fellow fugitives made themselves useful by guarding a large flock of sheep owned by Nabal.

One day David sent messengers to Nabal, asking if he could spare some provisions. Not only did Nabal refuse David's request, but he also taunted and humiliated the future king.

One of Nabal's servants overheard the exchange and ran to Abigail to tell her about it. She rushed into action to make up for her husband's foolishness. She gathered 200 loaves of bread, two wineskins full of wine, five slaughtered sheep, five seahs of parched grain, 100 clusters of raisins, and 200 fig cakes, and she rode out to deliver them to David.

She arrived just in time. David and his men were preparing to attack Nabal and his entire household. Abigail bowed to David and apologized for her husband's rude behavior. She asked for David's forgiveness and predicted that his descendants would rule Israel for generations.

Abigail's words—for her own household and for David's legacy—moved the future king to call off his attack.

Abigail returned home to find Nabal hosting a drunken party. The next morning, after he sobered up, she told him what she had done. Shocked, Nabal's "heart died within him, and he became as a stone." Ten days later, "the LORD struck Nabal and he died."

When David received word of Nabal's death, he seized the opportunity and asked Abigail to marry him. Abigail accepted his proposal, and, in so doing, this extraordinary woman became another wife of the future king of Israel.

Abigail, wife of David, 1873

42 The Medium of En-dor
(1 Samuel 28)

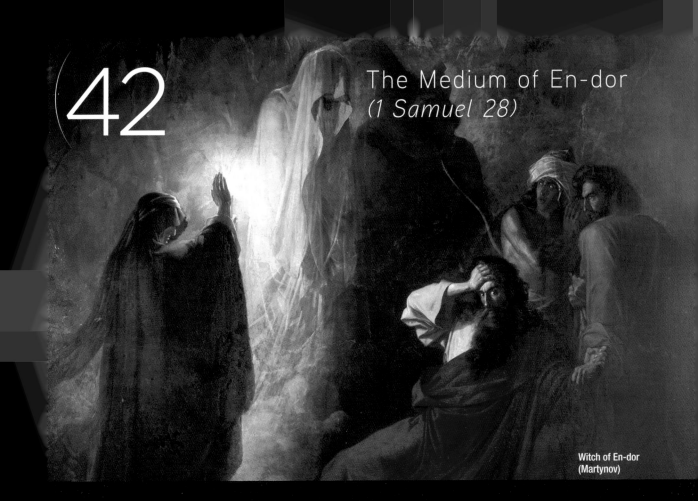

Witch of En-dor (Martynov)

itchcraft was illegal in Israel, punishable by death in the Torah, but King Saul himself had issued a decree banishing its practitioners from the kingdom. The decree had come from King Saul himself. So when the woman known as "the medium of En-dor" saw three men approaching her house, she must have been at least a little apprehensive. Every visit meant the possibility of arrest.

One of the men explained that he needed to speak to someone who had died.

The woman responded, "Surely you know what Saul has done, how he has cut off the mediums and the necromancers from the land. Why then are you laying a trap for my life to bring about my death?"

The man swore an oath that nothing bad would happen to her. He asked to speak to Samuel, the beloved prophet and priest of Israel who had recently died.

The medium of En-dor complied, summoning Samuel. When his spirit appeared, she screamed—not because the spirit scared her, but because she recognized the man sitting across from her as King Saul.

The king seemed desperate to talk to Samuel—desperate to receive a message from the LORD. According to the biblical passage, the spirit of Samuel obliged, but the message he offered only increased the king's desperation and agony.

Samuel told Saul that the LORD had taken the kingdom from him and given it to his rival, David. Furthermore, the LORD was going to give the army of Israel into the hands of the Philistines. Samuel told the king that his forces would face certain defeat. He warned Saul that he and his sons would face certain death.

Samuel's words were too much for Saul for to bear. Suddenly, the king of Israel fell to the ground, "filled with fear because of the words of Samuel." The medium of En-dor, no longer fearing for her life, rushed to help him. She got him to a bed and then prepared some meat and unleavened bread. She fed Saul and his servants, and they arose and went away that night.

43 Nathan
(2 Samuel 12)

Nathan served as the court prophet of King David. His task was to deliver messages from the LORD. In 2 Samuel 12, he was given a doozy. The LORD sent Nathan to confront King David about his adulterous affair with a woman named Bathsheba.

To cover up his affair—and Bathsheba's subsequent pregnancy—David had arranged to have his soldier, Uriah, Bathsheba's husband, killed in battle.

But King David didn't count on the prophet Nathan.

Surely Nathan considered the fact that David had already killed one man to prevent a scandal. Yet the prophet would not be dissuaded from delivering the message that God had given to him.

Nathan opted to deliver his message in the form of a story. He told David about a rich man who owned many sheep and cattle and a poor man who owned only one lamb. The poor man loved his lamb dearly and treated it as a family member.

One day a traveler visited the rich man's house. According to the custom of the day, the rich man prepared a lavish meal for his guest. Instead of using one of his own sheep or cattle, however, he killed the poor man's lamb and served it to his guest.

The king's reaction can be found in 2 Samuel 12:5–10:

> Then David's anger was greatly kindled against the man, and he said to Nathan, "As the Lord lives, the man who has done this deserves to die, and he shall restore the lamb fourfold, because he did this thing, and because he had no pity."
> Nathan said to David, "You are the man! Thus says the Lord, the God of Israel, 'I anointed you king over Israel, and I delivered you out of the hand of Saul. And I gave you your master's house and your master's wives into your arms and gave you the house of Israel and of Judah. And if this were too little, I would add to you as much more. Why have you despised the word of the Lord, to do what is evil in his sight? You have struck down Uriah the Hittite with the sword and have taken his wife to be your wife and have killed him with the sword of the Ammonites. Now therefore the sword shall never depart from your house, because you have despised me and have taken the wife of Uriah the Hittite to be your wife.'"

David immediately recognized the gravity of his sin and repented.

Relief from Madeleine Church in Paris, Prophet Nathan and King David, by M. Triqueti,1837.

Traditionally celebrated site of Absalom's tomb, Jerusalem

Absalom was the third son of David and a key player in the turmoil that rocked David's dysfunctiona family to its core. He was known for his long hair and his physical attractiveness.

Absalom's narrative in the book of 2 Samuel begins with the rape of his sister Tamar by his half-brother Amnon When David did nothing to punish Amnon or avenge Tamar Absalom took it upon himself to mete out justice. He invited Amnon to a feast and then had him killed.

After the killing, Absalom was forced to flee Jerusalem. He spent three years on the run. Eventually, Joab one of David's generals, was able to negotiate an uneasy peace between the two men.

Absalom returned to Jerusalem but assumed the role of usurper. He subverted his father's rule every chance he got. In the process, he gathered supporters o his own. Eventually, he led a rebellion against his father and managed to drive him from Jerusalem.

David gathered his forces and led them into battle against Absalom and his army. During the fighting, Absalom attempted to escape on a mule. His prized long, thick hair became entangled in the branches of a tree, leaving him suspended and vulnerable. Joab found him there and, even though David had commanded leniency for his son, the military commander killed Absalom with three javelins.

Absalom hanging on the oak tree by J. James Tissot. Illustration to book of Samuel (II), 18.9 :'And his head caught hold of the oak, and he was taken up between the heaven and the earth'. Third son of David, killed by hitting an oak tree at the Battle of Ephraim Wood. JJT: French painter, 15 October 1836 – 8 August 1902.

45 Shimei
(2 Samuel 16–19; 1 Kings 2)

After David was forced to flee Jerusalem during his son Absalom's rebellion, he assembled a group of followers and loyal warriors who were determined to restore him to the throne. The number of these followers grew exponentially until David had assembled a force that was powerful enough to challenge his son.

David made his way back to Jerusalem with his fighting force in tow. However, his triumphant return to the capital city was interrupted by curses and rocks. Shimei, a relative of Saul, hurled verbal abuse and physical stones at David and his army because he held David responsible for Saul's death.

> And he threw stones at David and at all the servants of King David, and all the people and all the mighty men were on his right hand and on his left. And Shimei said as he cursed, "Get out, get out, you man of blood, you worthless man! The LORD has avenged on you all the blood of the house of Saul, in whose place you have reigned, and the LORD has given the kingdom into the hand of your son Absalom. See, your evil is on you, for you are a man of blood." (2 Samuel 16:6–8)

David returned to Jerusalem, put down Absalom's rebellion, and reclaimed the throne. That was enough to prompt a change of heart in Shimei. He and his men came to David, sincerely apologized for their actions, and pledged their complete loyalty and cooperation to him. David absolved him for his actions at the time. However, when he was dying, he gave these instructions to Solomon regarding Shimei: "Now therefore do not hold him guiltless, for you are a wise man. You will know what you ought to do to him, and you shall bring his gray head down with blood to Sheol" (1 Kings 2:9).

So Solomon instructed Shimei to build a house in Jerusalem where he would remain, "for on the day you go out and cross the brook Kidron, know for certain that you shall die. Your blood shall be on your own head" (1 Kings 2:37).

Shimei agreed to Solomon's terms, but when his servants escaped to Gath, Shimei went after them. Solomon said to Shimei, "You know in your own heart all the harm that you did to David my father. So the LORD will bring back your harm on your own head" (1 Kings 2:44). Then Solomon ordered Shimei to be killed.

Shimei Curses David and His Men (2 Samuel 16), Illustration

46 Adonijah
(1 Kings 1–2)

Adonijah was the fourth son of King David and the second (after Absalom) to make a play for his father's throne. With his father on his deathbed, Adonijah set himself up to become king by parading through the streets of Jerusalem in a chariot, accompanied by horsemen and fifty men who ran before his chariot, announcing his coming.

Later he invited the king's other sons—all except Solomon—and some high-ranking priests (except Nathan the prophet) and military leaders to a celebratory sacrifice and feast. While he and his guests were making merry, word came that Solomon had been anointed king.

Adonijah panicked. He guessed that Solomon's first order of business as king would be to rid himself of challengers. Adonijah grabbed the altar in an effort to declare sanctuary for himself and escape his brother's wrath. Eventually, the two men met, and Solomon agreed to let Adonijah live. Not long afterward, King David died.

In the wake of his father's death, Adonijah approached Bathsheba, David's widow and Solomon's mother, to ask permission to marry Abishag, David's caretaker. For reasons that are not entirely clear or known, when Solomon learned what his half-brother had asked, he had Adonijah killed.

Solomon is anointed king

47 Solomon
(1 Kings 2–11)

Solomon faced the daunting task of succeeding his father David as king of Israel. According to 1 Kings 3, the LORD helped ease the transition when he appeared to Solomon in a dream. God told Solomon that anything he requested—wealth, long life, revenge on his enemies—would be given to him.

> And Solomon said, "You have shown great and steadfast love to your servant David my father, because he walked before you in faithfulness, in righteousness, and in uprightness of heart toward you. And you have kept for him this great and steadfast love and have given him a son to sit on his throne this day. And now, O LORD my God, you have made your servant king in place of David my father, although I am but a little child. I do not know how to go out or come in. And your servant is in the midst of your people whom you have chosen, a great people, too many to be numbered or counted for multitude. Give your servant therefore an understanding mind to govern your people, that I may discern between good and evil, for who is able to govern this your great people?" (1 Kings 3:6–9).

But Solomon's reign wasn't perfect, and he made many decisions that caused his downfall. First, he heavily taxed the people of Israel, and they weren't happy about it. Second, he accumulated an excessive number of foreign wives (700 of them!), which helped turn his heart away from the LORD to the worship of idols. This was God's response to Solomon:

> "Since this has been your practice and you have not kept my covenant and my statutes that I have commanded you, I will surely tear the kingdom from you and will give it to your servant. Yet for the sake of David your father I will not do it in your days, but I will tear it out of the hand of

your son. However, I will not tear away all the kingdom, but I will give one tribe to your son, for the sake of David my servant and for the sake of Jerusalem that I have chosen." (1 Kings 11: 11–13)

Solomon's indiscretions certainly had far-reaching consequences for the people of Israel, yet Solomon leaves behind a legacy that can't be denied. He built the long-awaited temple in Jerusalem. The Bible says

that he amassed one of the greatest fortunes in ancient history. He established a reputation as one of the wisest and most incisive men who ever lived. According to 1 Kings 4:34, "People of all nations came to hear the wisdom of Solomon, and from all the kings of the earth, who had heard of his wisdom."

Several books are traditionally attributed to Solomon: Song of Solomon, Ecclesiastes, and most of the book of Proverbs. The book of Ecclesiastes is traditionally considered a record of his reflections over his life and the wrong choices he made. After listing all the wealth and wisdom he had acquired, he had this to say: "Then I considered all that my hands had done and the toil I had expended in doing it, and behold, all was vanity and a striving after wind, and there was nothing to be gained under the sun" (Ecclesiastes 2:11).

Luca Giordano -
Dream of Solomon

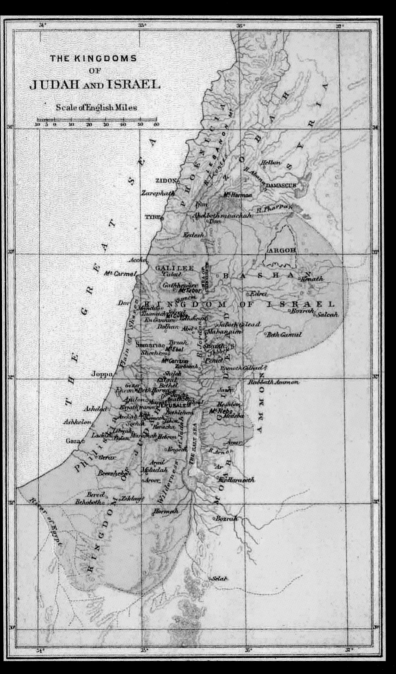

THE KINGDOMS
OF
JUDAH AND ISRAEL.

Scale of English Miles

Maacah could boast of a personal relationship to the first three kings of Judah. She was married to King Rehoboam, the son of Solomon. When Solomon's kingdom split in two, Rehoboam became the first ruler of the southern kingdom of Judah.

Like his father, Rehoboam allowed idolatry to flourish throughout his kingdom. Also like his father, Rehoboam had many wives. Yet he prized Maacah above them all.

When Abijah assumed the throne, his mother, Maacah, assumed the title of queen mother. Abijah's reign resembled that of his father. He allowed idol worship in Judah. His reign lasted only three years.

The throne of Judah passed to Abijah's son (and Maacah's grandson) Asa. In the succession, Maacah retained her position as queen mother, but only for a short time. Asa worshiped the LORD exclusively. He banished all shrines and idols from Judah—starting with those made close to home.

According to 1 Kings 15:13, Maacah had made an image of Asherah, an idol associated with a Canaanite deity. Asa deposed his idol-worshiping grandmother.

Map of the ancient kingdoms
of Judah and Israel.

49 Elijah
(1 Kings 18)

And then there was one.

King Ahab and Queen Jezebel (a Phoenician princess) had done everything in their power to rid Israel of the prophets of the Lord. They killed as many as they could, and many went into hiding. The royal couple followed the Canaanite gods, Baal and Asherah.

Only the prophet Elijah remained to oppose Ahab and Jezebel. Elijah had an especially big target on his back because he had announced divine judgment on Israel. Shortly thereafter, a severe drought gripped the land, devastating Israel's food and water supply. King Ahab blamed Elijah.

Elijah was not intimidated. He challenged the prophets of Baal and Asherah to a contest. Two altars would be built: one to Elijah's God and one to the god Baal. The first deity to send fire to consume the sacrifice on his altar would be declared the God of Israel.

Four hundred and fifty prophets of Baal prepared their wooden altar and sacrifice. When everything was ready, they began to call upon Baal. From morning until after midday, they pleaded with Baal to send a fire. They danced and shouted. They cut themselves with swords and spears, all to no avail.

The eyes of the nation turned to Elijah. His first step was to repair the altar of the Lord with twelve stones, since it had been torn down. His next step was to dig a trench, deep enough to hold about three and a half gallons of water, around the altar. He covered the top of the altar with firewood, cut up his bull for sacrifice, and placed the meat on top of the wood.

With everything in place, Elijah handed out four water jars and instructed people to fill them with water and pour it over his sacrifice and altar—not once, not twice, but three times. Twelve pots of water drenched the meat, the wood, and the altar. The runoff filled the trench.

Elijah offered his own prayer: "O Lord, God of Abraham, Isaac, and Israel, let it be known this day that you are God in Israel, and that I am your servant, and that I have done all these things at your word. Answer

ROME, ITALY: The prophet Elijah marble statue by Raffaello da Montelupo (1522) in the Chigi chapel in the Basilica di Santa Maria del Popolo.

me, O Lord, answer me, that this people may know that you, O Lord, are God, and that you have turned their hearts back" (1 Kings 18:36–37).

Fire roared from heaven to consume Elijah's offering, the stones of the altar, the dust, and every drop of water in the trench.

"When all the people saw it, they fell on their faces and said, 'The Lord, he is God; the Lord, he is God'" (1 Kings 18:39).

50 Elisha
(2 Kings 2–14)

Elisha was plowing his father's fields when he first encountered Elijah. The young Elisha dropped everything to follow the respected prophet. For years, he watched Elijah perform his duties. He absorbed the example set by his mentor. And when Elijah departed—via a whirlwind, accompanied by fiery chariots, according to 2 Kings 2:11—Elisha stepped into the role as a prophet of the LORD.

Some time later, the people of Jericho approached Elisha with a life-threatening situation. The water of the area was causing sickness and preventing crops from growing. Elisha poured salt into a nearby spring and pronounced God's blessing on it. The water became pure, according to 2 Kings 2:22.

As he left Jericho, a group of boys hurled insults at Elisha. Second Kings 2:24 states that after Elisha pronounced a curse on them in the name of the LORD, two she-bears attacked the boys, tearing forty-two of them.

When the kings of Israel, Judah, and Edom joined together to battle the Moabites, they turned to Elisha because their soldiers had no water to drink. Elisha told the kings that the streambed would fill with water. He also rebuked the king of Israel.

The narrative of 2 Kings suggests that God used Elisha in miraculous ways. When a widow of one of the "sons of the prophets" told Elisha that creditors were going to take her sons because of her late husband's unpaid debts, Elisha gave her instructions that turned one small pot of oil into a surplus that she could sell.

When an elderly couple's young son suddenly died, Elisha prayed to the LORD and laid on the boy's body until he came back to life. When Naaman, a foreign military commander, was stricken with a skin disease, Elisha healed him by instructing him to dip himself in the Jordan River seven times.

Elisha served as a prophet for sixty-five years.

51 Jezebel
(1 Kings 16, 18, and 21)

Born into privilege, Jezebel was a Phoenician princess, the daughter of Ethbaal, the king of Tyre. As a young woman, Jezebel married Ahab, the king of Israel. Ahab served the gods Baal and Asherah. King Ahab is considered by the book of Kings to have angered the Lord more than any other Israelite king.

Ahab and Jezebel ushered in a new era of idol worship in Israel, making Baal worship the major religion of the entire northern kingdom, but Jezebel didn't stop there.

The queen of Israel led a persecution of the prophets of the Lord. She killed many of them and the rest went into hiding, until only the prophet Elijah remained. She imported 850 prophets of Baal and Asherah to fill their roles.

When Elijah exposed Jezebel's prophets as frauds and turned the people of Israel against them, the queen was furious. She vowed to have Elijah killed.

No one was safe from Jezebel's wickedness. One of her subjects, a man named Naboth, refused to sell his vineyard to the king, as was the king's right. Jezebel arranged to have Naboth falsely accused of blasphemy and stoned to death. Ahab took possession of his vineyard.

Jezebel's rule came to an end when King Ahab was killed in battle. An army commander named Jehu was given the task of destroying the king's descendants, as well as his wicked queen.

When Jezebel heard that Jehu had arrived, she put on make-up and did her hair. Jehu called to her own servants to throw her down, and a few of them grabbed her and threw her from the window to her death.

Baal temple in Palmyre, Syria

52 Athaliah
(2 Kings 11)

A thaliah was the daughter of King Ahab, who is regarded in the Bible as one of the most wicked rulers in Israel's history. Scholars debate whether her mother was Queen Jezebel or another, unnamed wife of Ahab.

Athaliah married King Jehoram of Judah—a union that united the kingdom of Israel and the kingdom of Judah for the first time in many years. After her husband was killed, Athaliah's son Ahaziah inherited the throne. Some Bible scholars have suggested that Athaliah held on to her royal position by becoming one of her son's most trusted advisers—perhaps even the power behind the throne.

Not only did Athaliah outlive her husband, but she outlived her son as well. Desperate to hold on to her power, she launched a bloodbath to eliminate all potential successors to the throne.

She managed to kill all but one, a grandson named Joash, who was hidden away in the temple until he was old enough to assume the throne. In the interval, Athaliah reigned as Israel's monarch for six years.

Her tenure was interrupted by the reemergence of her grandson Joash, as the people of Israel rallied around the rightful king. When Athaliah tried to quash their rebellion, they executed her.

Athaliah, queen of Judah,
dragged from the temple, artist unknown, Paris, France.

53 Jehosheba
(2 Kings 11)

Evil seemed to run rampant in the royal court of the kingdom of Judah following the death of King Ahaziah. Athaliah—the mother of Ahaziah and queen mother of Judah—refused to allow anyone else to inherit her son's throne or challenge her authority. The matriarch ordered the massacre of the royal family. By eliminating her rivals, Athaliah hoped to solidify her own position as the ruler of Judah.

Her scheme may have worked, if not for the intervention of a princess named Jehosheba.

Jehosheba managed to rescue one of her nephews, a young boy named Joash. She hid Joash away in the temple, where her husband served as a priest. For six years Jehosheba secretly sheltered the boy, who was Athaliah's grandson, at tremendous risk to herself.

Athaliah never found out. For six years, she ruled over Judah. Meanwhile, Joash, the true heir to the throne, was prepared for his emergence. They waited until the time was right and then brought him out under heavy guard. When the people of Judah discovered who he was, they immediately threw their support behind Joash, the rightful king.

Athaliah tried to end the uprising, but the people turned on her and killed her. Joash became king and immediately set to work undoing the evil deeds of his predecessors. He was able to save Judah because Jehosheba cared enough to save him.

Queen Athaliah orders the king's children to be killed, Harmen Jansz Muller, Hadrianus Junius, Gerard de Jode, 1565-1569

54 Hezekiah
(2 Kings 18–20; 2 Chronicles 29–33; Isaiah 36–39)

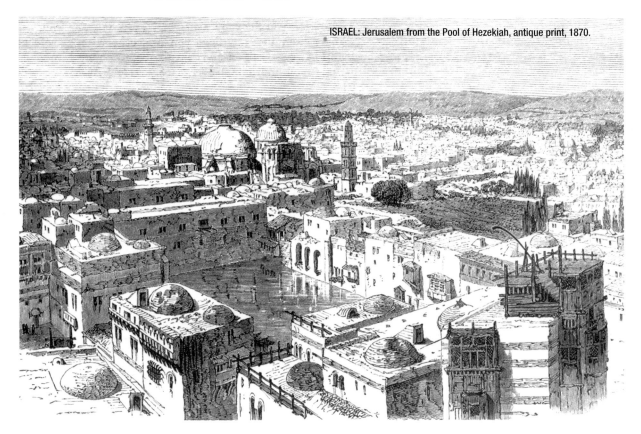

ISRAEL: Jerusalem from the Pool of Hezekiah, antique print, 1870.

Hezekiah ranks near the top of the best-loved and most effective kings in Jewish history. The son of King Ahaz, Hezekiah ruled the southern kingdom of Judah for twenty-nine years.

Hezekiah's distinguishing characteristic for the biblical writers was his faithfulness to the Lord. According to the Chronicler, one of his first acts as king was to reopen the temple in Jerusalem and remove the idols that had been installed there. The priests and Levites were instructed to perform their duties according to the specifications of ancient Jewish law. In Chronicles, Hezekiah reached out to the people of the northern kingdom of Israel and invited them to join the people of Judah for Passover at the temple.

The king had to walk a fine political line. His father had made an alliance with the Assyrians that made Judah a vassal state. When the king of Assyria died, Hezekiah rebelled, trying to reestablish Judah's independence. In doing so, he incurred the wrath of the new Assyrian king, Sennacherib.

Hezekiah prepared Judah for the inevitable Assyrian attack by rebuilding city walls, raising towers, and forging weapons and shields. When the Assyrian army attacked Judah, Hezekiah apologized and offered to pay tribute. However, even though he stripped the temple of its silver and gold to make the payment, Sennacherib still continued his plan of attack. Hezekiah prayed in the temple for his God's intervention. According to 2 Kings 19:35, the angel of the Lord killed 185,000 Assyrians that night. Sennacherib and his army returned home to Nineveh.

55 Tiglath-Pileser
(2 Kings 15, 16)

One of the recurring themes of the Old Testament books of prophecy is the destruction of the northern kingdom of Israel. The prophets Joel, Amos, Hosea, and Micah all warned that the Lord would bring judgment on the kingdom because the Israelites had forsaken his law, worshiped idols, and allowed injustice to flourish.

When the long-threatened judgment finally came, it came in the form of Tiglath-Pileser. This Assyrian king was determined to expand his kingdom. He attacked cities in Syria and Philistia before his attention was turned to the northern kingdom of Israel.

Menahem, the king of Israel, squeezed huge sums from the wealthy men of Israel to offer as a tribute to Tiglath-Pileser, hoping it would keep the foreign king from attacking. The Assyrian king withdrew, but eventually returned when King Ahaz of Judah became his vassal in exchange for Assyria attacking his enemies, Pekah of Israel and Rezin of Syria. Tiglath-Pileser accepted Judah's vassalage and attacked Damascus before turning against Pekah, the new king of Israel, who was ultimately helpless to resist. Tiglath-tPileser's successor, Shalmaneser V (and maybe Sargon II), conquered Israel and deported its people to Assyria.

In doing so, according to the narrative of 2 Kings, the Assyrian armies fulfilled God's prophesied judgment on Israel.

Tiglath-Pileser III before the citadel of Turushpa, capital of the Kingdom of Urartu, after his unsuccessful siege of the city in 735 BC. Tiglath-Pileser III, king of Assyria in the eighth century BCE, introduced advanced civil, military, and political systems into the Neo-Assyrian Empire. After the painting by Margaret Dovaston, (1884-1954). From Hutchinson's History of the Nations, published 1915.

(56 Hosea
(Hosea 1–14)

Hosea likely was a contemporary of the Old Testament prophets Isaiah, Amos, and Micah. Yet as far as the Bible indicates, none of them ever received the instruction that Hosea received:

"Go, take to yourself a wife of whoredom and have children of whoredom" (Hosea 1:2).

According to Hosea 1:2, the instruction came from the Lord, who was determined to give the people of Israel a stark image of their relationship with him. The woman Hosea married was named Gomer. In her unconventional relationship with the prophet, she represented Israel; Hosea represented God.

Gomer bore Hosea three children. In her discretion, the people of Israel were meant to see their own spiritual adultery—that is, their pursuit of other gods.

When the LORD instructed Hosea to bring Gomer back home, her illicit lover demanded money for her return. Her faithful husband Hosea paid her ransom, brought her home, and loved her. His selfless actions illustrated God's love for his unfaithful people.

Hosea endured the heartache of an adulterous spouse, but he obeyed God in order to help his fellow Israelites return and be faithful to their God.

CORDOBA, SPAIN: A fresco of the prophet Hosea by Cristobal Vela and Juan Luis Zambrano in the church Iglesia de San Augustin, 17th Century.

Gomer was a prostitute in ancient Israel. Imagine her surprise when Hosea, a prophet of the Lord, proposed marriage to her. The prophet knew the life she lived, yet he loved her anyway.

The two married and began a life together. Gomer gave birth to three children: two boys and a girl.

Despite her marriage vows to Hosea, she returned to her former trade and again took several lovers. God instructed Hosea to take his wife back. "Go again, love a woman who is loved by another man and an adulteress," the LORD said to Hosea.

Hosea bought back Gomer from her lover for fifteen pieces of silver, five bushels of barley, and a measure of wine. Hosea redeemed his wife, took her back to their home, and loved her.

The book of Hosea explains that in pairing Hosea with Gomer, God called attention to the dysfunctional relationship between himself and Israel. God was the spurned husband and Israel the unfaithful wife. The people of Israel involved themselves with other gods the way Gomer involved herself with her lovers. Hosea describes how, rather than turning his back on his

unfaithful people, God still loved them and would bring them back to enjoy his blessings.

Hosea and Gomer

Jonah and the whale

58 Jonah
(Jonah 1–4)

Jonah stands alone among the prophets of the Old Testament as the only person the Bible records as refusing an assignment from the Lord. His assignment was to warn the people of Nineveh that their wickedness offended God.

Jonah wanted nothing to do with the task—not because he was afraid of the Ninevites but because he was afraid they would respond positively to his message. Nineveh was the capital city of Assyria, Israel's bitter enemy. Jonah reasoned that if the Ninevites were receptive to God's warning, they would repent and escape God's wrath. If, on the other hand, they continued to offend God, eventually God would send a devastating punishment on them. And that's just what Jonah wanted.

Jonah booked passage on a boat bound for Tarshish—and away from Nineveh. He didn't get far. The vessel encountered foul weather as soon as it hit the open sea. The boat's crewmen claimed a divine judgment was at work.

Jonah admitted he was the reason for the storm and urged them to throw him overboard. The sailors resisted at first, but eventually they tossed Jonah into the sea to save themselves.

The waters calmed immediately, and a giant fish swallowed the renegade prophet. Jonah 1:17 says Jonah spent three days and three nights in the fish's stomach. Eventually the fish vomited Jonah back on shore. Jonah headed for Nineveh.

The prophet walked through the city proclaiming that God's judgment would occur in forty days unless the Ninevites repented. According to Jonah 3:5, "The people of Nineveh believed God. They called for a fast and put on sackcloth, from the greatest of them to the least of them." Fasting and wearing sackcloth were ways of demonstrating humility and repentance.

Just as the prophet had feared, the Lord "relented of the disaster that he had said he would do to them, and he did not do it" (3:10).

The biblical writer wants to show that the one who delivered Israel from bondage in Egypt is ready to offer deliverance to anyone who turns away from evil and toward God. This is why the book of Jonah has been read for centuries in Jewish synagogues worldwide on the Day of Atonement (Yom Kippur), the most solemn Jewish holiday of the year.

(59) Isaiah
(Isaiah 1–66)

King Uzziah came and went, as did Kings Jotham, Ahaz, and Hezekiah. Yet throughout more than six decades of upheaval and uncertainty in Judah, one constant remained. The prophet Isaiah faithfully delivered the messages of the Lord to the rulers and people of the kingdom.

The Bible offers few personal details about Isaiah beyond the name of his father, Amoz. Isaiah's access to the court of King Uzziah suggests that he may have been related to the king, or perhaps was a court prophet. The language, rhetorical devices, and literary imagery found in his words suggest that he was highly educated. He was married to a woman who is described as a "prophetess" (Isaiah 8:3). It's not known whether she served as a prophet in her own right or whether the title refers to her status as a prophet's wife.

What is known is that Isaiah fulfilled his prophetic responsibilities with boldness and imagination. His words were often polarizing, but they were never dull.

The era in which he prophesied was fraught with turmoil. When Isaiah began his ministry, Judah was materially wealthy but filled with greed and injustice. He spoke out against the people's religiosity and arrogance and against their leaders' indifference to injustice. He warned of impending judgment.

Isaiah's words fell on deaf ears. Corruption ran rampant during the reign of Ahaz. The narrative of Isaiah suggests that the king's refusal to consult the Lord before his ill-considered military alliances and campaigns led to Judah becoming a vassal state of Assyria. Isaiah warned that judgment would follow and urged the king to turn back to God.

To demonstrate the foolishness of relying on alliances with nations such as

Egypt, the Lord instructed Isaiah to remove his traditional sackcloth clothing and walk around naked and barefoot. Isaiah did as he was instructed. In fact, Isaiah always did as he was instructed by the Lord.

Prophet Isaiah (Isaias) statue in Rome, Italy. located at the famous Spanish Square (Piazza di Spagna).

(60 Huldah
(2 Kings 22)

The Hebrew handwritten Torah, on a synagogue altar, illustrating Jewish holidays.

According to the Bible, the kingdom of Judah was not adhering to the Law before Josiah became king. In fact, most Israelites were unaware of their religious laws. When the Book of the Law was discovered in the temple of Jerusalem, they must have seemed like strange, ancient artifacts to the people.

Josiah demanded that the newly discovered Book of the Law be read aloud to him. What he heard distressed him. The Bible indicates that he came face-to-face with the wrath of the Lord that Judah's disobedience had stirred up.

The desperate king sent a delegation to Huldah to find out just how dire the situation was. She was the wife of Shallum, who was an official in the palace. She was also a prophetess in Jerusalem.

Huldah's response confirmed Josiah's fears that the LORD was going to punish Judah soon because of the corruption of the people. But she also delivered a ray of hope to Josiah, that since he had repented, he would die in peace and not see the disaster planned for Judah.

It was after hearing her prophecy that Josiah gathered all the people of Israel to read the Book of the Law, and renewed the covenant in the presence of the Lord.

61 Daniel
(Daniel 1–6)

Daniel was a young man when Judah fell to the Babylonians. Like other strong and capable young people in Judah, Daniel was carried away into captivity in Babylon. There, he made a powerful impression on key government officials. When the Babylonian Empire gave way to the Persian Empire, Daniel made a similar impression on Persian officials.

Specifically, he made a name for himself as an adviser to King Darius. Daniel's quick rise to prominence inspired jealousy among the king's other advisers. They schemed to get rid of him, targeting his adherence to his Jewish religion as his vulnerable spot.

Daniel's political enemies convinced Darius to issue a decree that said for the next thirty days, any person who prayed to anyone, god or man, except the king would be thrown into the lions' den. The king signed the decree into law, not realizing that Daniel prayed three times a day to his God—in front of an open window that faced Jerusalem.

Daniel fully understood the danger he faced. Still, he went to his room, dropped to his knees, and prayed to his God in full view of his enemies, who were keeping a watchful eye on him.

Bound by his own decree, King Darius was forced to throw Daniel into a pit of lions and seal the pit with a stone. The next morning, he rushed back to the site. Daniel 6:20–22 picks up the story:

> As [King Darius] came near to the den where Daniel was, he cried out in a tone of anguish. The king declared to Daniel, "O Daniel, servant of the living God, has your God, whom you serve continually, been able to deliver you from the lions?" Then Daniel said to the king, "O king, live forever! My God sent his angel and shut the lions' mouths, and they have not harmed me, because I was found blameless before him; and also before you, O king, I have done no harm."

According to the book of Daniel, the incident had a powerful impact on the king, who issued another decree, compelling his people to tremble and fear before the God Daniel served.

62 Shadrach, Meshach, and Abednego
(Daniel 3)

Shadrach, Meshach, and Abednego were young Jewish men who were captives in Babylon. Despite their status as exiles, all three worked their way into positions of influence as advisers to Nebuchadnezzar, the king of Babylon.

Their good standing with the king was threatened when Nebuchadnezzar erected a ninety-foot-tall gold statue of himself and ordered everyone in his kingdom to bow down and worship it. Forbidden by Jewish religious law from bowing to idols, Shadrach, Meshach, and Abednego refused to obey the king's command.

The enraged king issued an ultimatum: "Fall down and worship the statue that I have made. . . . But if you do not, you shall immediately be cast into a burning fiery

furnace. And who is the god who will deliver you out of my hands?" (Daniel 3:15).

The three faithful Israelites would not be cowed. "O Nebuchadnezzar, we have no need to answer you in this matter. If this be so, our God whom we serve is able to deliver us from the burning fiery furnace, and he will deliver us out of your hand, O king. But if not, be it known to you, O king, that we will not serve your gods or worship the golden image that you have set up" (Daniel 3:16–18).

Their faithfulness to their God could not be shaken—not even by the prospect of a painful death.

Nebuchadnezzar gave orders to stoke the furnace seven times hotter than normal. The heat was so intense that the men who carried Shadrach, Meshach, and Abednego to the furnace's opening were killed instantly. The three Israelites, on the other hand, were able to walk around, unharmed, inside the furnace. According to Daniel 3:25, they weren't alone.

Nebuchadnezzar saw a fourth man in the furnace, one who looked "like a son of the gods." The king called for Shadrach, Meshach, and Abednego to come out. Not a single hair on their head or thread on their clothes had been singed.

King Nebuchadnezzar quickly changed his tune. He said,

Blessed be the God of Shadrach, Meshach, and Abednego, who has sent his angel and delivered his servants, who trusted in him, and set aside the king's command, and yielded up their bodies rather than serve and worship any god except their own God. Therefore I make a decree: Any people, nation, or language that speaks anything against the God of Shadrach, Meshach, and Abednego shall be torn limb from limb, and their houses laid in ruins, for there is no other god who is able to rescue in this way. (Daniel 3:28–29)

Shadrach, Meshach, and Abednego in the fiery furnace - Picture from The Holy Scriptures, Old and New Testaments books collection published in 1885, Stuttgart-Germany. Drawings by Gustave Dore.

63 Ezekiel
(Ezekiel 1–48)

Ezekiel stained glass, All Saints Church, Swinford, Leicestershire, England, UK

Ezekiel emerged as a spokesperson for the LORD during an especially low period in Judah's history. The Babylonians had deposed Jerusalem's king, Jehoiachin, and carried away about 10,000 inhabitants to serve in Babylon. The Jewish exiles were forced to live in settlements in Babylon. Ezekiel conducted his prophetic ministry from one such settlement.

Ezekiel went to great lengths to communicate the messages he was given by God. He once built a model of the city of Jerusalem under siege. Another time he lay on his left side for 390 days and then lay on his right side for another 40 days. He also cut off his beard, burned one-third of his whiskers, cut one-third of them with a sword, and scattered one-third of them to the wind.

As was the case with most prophets in the Bible, Ezekiel saw his messages ignored and rejected. His audience was already miserable and homesick. The last thing they wanted to hear was that they were to blame for their circumstances.

All was not doom and gloom with Ezekiel, however. The prophet offered words of hope to his fellow Jewish exiles. He assured them that their God had not abandoned them and that their punishment was only temporary.

Ezekiel was one of the few prophets who was also a priest. The commands to bear the punishment of his people (Ezekiel 4:4–6) and avoid mourning his wife's death (Ezekiel 24:15–27) are commands given to priests. He is also the only prophet to carry out his ministry entirely outside of Israel. Because of his emphasis on teaching, Jewish tradition credits Ezekiel with encouraging the exiles to build synagogues and houses of Torah study in Babylon, to keep the spirit of Judaism alive.

64 Zerubbabel, Ezra, and Nehemiah
(Ezra 1–10; Nehemiah 1–13)

In 586 BC, the Babylonians laid waste to Jerusalem. The invaders left no structure undamaged. They destroyed Solomon's Temple, as well as the walls that surrounded and protected the city. For decades, the city lay in ruins while its people were held captive by the Babylonians— until the rise of Persia.

While they were in exile, the Judahites begged the Lord to restore their kingdom. The book of Ezra suggests that God answered their prayers by softening the hearts of their captors. Around 536 BCE, a man named Zerubbabel secured permission from Cyrus, the king of Persia, to lead a group of Jewish exiles back to Jerusalem. Their purpose was to rebuild the temple of Jerusalem, the center of religious life for the Jewish people. The exiles completed their task in a little over twenty years.

Around 458 BCE, a priest named Ezra secured permission from the Persian king Darius to lead a second group of Jewish exiles back to Jerusalem.

Around fourteen years after Ezra's group returned to Jerusalem, a royal cupbearer named Nehemiah learned that the returnees had no protection from their enemies because the walls of Jerusalem were still in ruins. Nehemiah explained the situation to his master, the Persian king Artaxerxes. Artaxerxes gave Nehemiah permission—and supplies—to lead yet another group of exiles back to Jerusalem to rebuild the city's walls.

The surrounding nations saw Nehemiah's mission as a threat. The last thing the Samaritans, Ammonites, and Philistines wanted was for Jerusalem to become militarily secure again. Nehemiah and his workers paid little heed to their objections—though occasionally they worked with a tool in one hand and a weapon in the other, just to be safe.

The leader of the Samaritans accused Nehemiah of plotting a rebellion against Persia. He persuaded some Jewish nobles and prophets to oppose the building project. Nehemiah didn't waver. He completed construction of the walls in fifty-two days.

Zerubbabel, Ezra, and Nehemiah were instrumental in rebuilding Jerusalem.

65 Vashti
(Esther 1)

Ahasuerus, the king of Persia (also known as Xerxes), threw an epic banquet for certain men in his kingdom. As per royal custom, his queen, Vashti, hosted an equally epic banquet for their wives. For an entire week, the two parties raged in separate areas of the palace. After seven days of drinking, the men's celebration got a little out of hand.

King Ahasuerus sent for Vashti. She was a beautiful woman and the king wanted to show her off to his guests, "for she was lovely to look at." The king was asking her to degrade herself to satisfy his ego and whim.

Vashti refused the king's request. Ahasuerus was stunned. He had to consult his advisers regarding his options.

The Trailblazer

Vashti's refusal to parade herself for King Ahasuerus's pleasure was cited by Harriet Beecher Stowe, the author of *Uncle Tom's Cabin*, as the "first stand for women's rights."

"According to the law, what is to be done to Queen Vashti," he demanded, "because she has not performed the command of King Ahasuerus delivered by the eunuchs?"

The king's advisers were just as shaken for a different reason. The Bible indicates that they were concerned Vashti's example would inspire the wives of noble Persian and Median households to disrespect their husbands.

The decision was made to banish Queen Vashti from the king's presence forever and to give her royal position to another. This, according to the book of Esther, would prompt the women of the Persian Empire to honor their husbands.

66 Haman
(Esther 1–7)

There are villains, and then there are power-hungry tyrants who respond to perceived slights by planning to murder an entire people group. Haman falls squarely into the second category.

Haman was an official in the court of King Ahasuerus. As a top official, the king had commanded his servants, who gathered at the city gates, to bow down to him. One of those servants—Mordecai, a Jewish exile living in Persia—refused to bow to Haman.

Haman plotted a revengeful scheme that was extreme by any standard. He convinced King Ahasuerus that the Jewish people in Persia refused to obey the king's laws. Haman recommended executing all of them. He even offered to pay 10,000 talents of silver to the king in order to make it happen. The incentive was enough to convince the king to issue the edict. Haman set about building special gallows especially for Mordecai.

But Haman didn't realize that Esther, the king's beloved queen, was not only Jewish herself but also the orphaned cousin/adopted daughter of Mordecai. According to the book of Esther, by appealing to the king and through the coincidence that Mordecai had once saved the life of the king, the tables were turned on Haman.

In the end, justice was served. The Jews were saved, and King Ahasuerus ordered that Haman be hanged from the gallows he had created for Mordecai. Mordecai and Esther established a holiday to commemorate these amazing events. Jews worldwide celebrate on the fourteenth of Adar (February or March in the Solar or Gregorian Calendar). This holiday, called "Purim," is the most joyous holiday in the Jewish calendar.

Still Celebrated

The Jewish holiday of Purim commemorates the deliverance of the Jews from Haman's evil plan to exterminate them. Part of the celebration involves reading aloud the scroll of Esther.

Haman accused by Queen Esther of plotting to kill the Persian Jews. Haman the Agagite described in the old testament, Book of Esther, as vizier in the Persian empire under King Ahasuerus,(Xerxes I).

67 Mordecai
(Esther 1–10)

Mordecai was a Jewish exile living in Persia, who stepped in when his young cousin Hadassah was orphaned. He adopted the girl and raised her as his own. He secretly advised her when Ahasuerus, the king of Persia, chose her to be his queen. Hadassah is better known as Queen Esther.

Mordecai uncovered a plot to assassinate the king and acted quickly to make the plan known and save Ahasuerus's life. Mordecai refused to bow to a petty tyrant in the king's court named Haman. In doing so, he triggered in Haman a psychotic quest for revenge. Mordecai's new enemy devised a plan to execute—with the king's approval—all the Jews in the Persian Empire.

Mordecai convinced Esther to appeal to King Ahasuerus, and she thwarted Haman's scheme. She went toe-to-toe with one of the most cunning political creatures in Persia and beat him at his own game. In addition to rescuing a child and saving the life of a king, Mordecai prevented genocide.

Bible Illustration of the triumph of Mordecai. By Gustave Dore

68 Esther
(Esther 4)

After Queen Vashti was removed for refusing to appear before King Ahasuerus (also known as Xerxes), Ahasuerus selected a young woman named Esther to replace Vashti, after she won what amounted to a beauty pageant.

Esther does not appear to be easily intimidated. Haman, an official whose wounded pride led him to plan genocide against the Jews, was a formidable political adversary. He knew how to manipulate the law—and the king—for his own gain. Yet Esther, once convinced by Mordecai, did not back down from him. She outmaneuvered Haman so deftly that he never even anticipated her final move.

Esther used her influence, power, and authority to help others. Like an experienced government official, she expended her political capital when it was needed most. As queen, she was one of the few who had the clout to summon King Ahasuerus and Haman to a royal banquet.

Esther was willing to risk everything for the greater good of her people. Her simple act of visiting the king in

Esther leaving King Ahasuerus'/ Xerxes' presence. She was chosen to replace his wife, Vashti, as Queen of Persia (Esther). Illustration by Philip R. Morris (1836-1902).

his inner court without an invitation was punishable by death. Esther risked her life to get Ahasuerus's attention.

She risked it again when she identified herself to the king as a Jew—even though, by law, being a Jew put her under the death sentence engineered by Haman.

Esther had no guarantee that her plan would work—or even that she would survive its execution. She knew only that her people were in trouble and that she had the means to help them.

(69) Joseph, the Husband of Mary
(Matthew 1–2; Luke 2)

Though he is a minor character in the Gospel narratives, Joseph emerges as a deeply honorable man. The Gospel of Matthew shows how he stood beside Mary during her pregnancy, despite the perhaps inevitable gossip and attacks on his character and hers since they were betrothed but the marriage contract not completed. So, "Joseph, being a just man and unwilling to put her to shame, resolved to divorce her quietly" (Matthew 1:19). He risked his reputation and standing in the community for the sake of a plan that was explained to him in a dream by an "angel of the Lord" (Matthew 1:20). Matthew says he took Mary as his wife "but knew her not until she had given birth to a son" (1:25).

Joseph is clearly the protector of the young family since twice more, Matthew 2 notes, an angel of the Lord addresses him in dreams: first to take his family and flee to Egypt to escape a murderous King Herod, and second to return home with his family after Herod's death. While returning, he hears that one of Herod's sons, Archelaus, is now reigning, and being fearful of him, Joseph settles in Nazareth in the district of Galilee.

Further glimpses of Joseph's character and influence is seen other Gospel passages.

The Gospel of Luke indicates that in the town of Bethlehem, overrun with taxpayers and leaving no guest room for Joseph and his pregnant wife, Mary, he managed to secure lodging, even if it was with the animals.

In another instance, Luke notes that on the way home from a Passover trip to Jerusalem, Joseph and Mary discovered that twelve-year-old Jesus wasn't in their caravan, already a day out from Jerusalem. Joseph and Mary searched among their relatives and kept searching for him. Joseph's fatherly concern for Jesus is apparent. They eventually arrived in Jerusalem and found Jesus in the temple.

When his parents saw him, they were astonished. And his mother said to him, "Son, why have you treated us so? Behold, your father and I have been searching for you in great distress." And he said to them, "Why were you looking for me? Did you not know that I must be in my Father's house?" (Luke 2:48–49)

The Gospels of Matthew and Mark refer to Joseph as ὁ τέκτονος/ὁ τέκτων, a craftsman who builds with and makes things with wood, sometimes stone or metal. In that culture, it is entirely likely that Joseph spent hours with Jesus in his workshop and out on jobs, teaching him the skills he could use to make a living. Even when Jesus returned to Nazareth years later, the people there still remembered him as "the carpenter's son" (Matthew 13:55; Mark 6:3). In their minds, Jesus's identity was still linked to Joseph and his family.

70 Mary, the Mother of Jesus
(Luke 1)

To be chosen as the mother of a son who would be "great and . . . called the Son of the Most High" and to whom the Lord God would give "the throne of his father David" (Luke 1:32) would have been the highest calling imaginable to a woman in first-century Israel. Why the honor fell to Mary, a betrothed virgin (1:27–34) is one of the great mysteries of the gospel narrative.

Perhaps it was Mary's humble nature. According to Luke's Gospel, she was troubled by the angel Gabriel's salutation—"Greetings, O favored one, the Lord is with you!"—and message. What might it mean? How could she conceive a son since, "I am still a virgin?" (1:34).

Perhaps it was Mary's spirit of service. When she heard from the angel what God planned to do, her response was, "Behold, I am the servant of the Lord, let it be to me according to your word" (1:38).

Perhaps it was Mary's spirit of joy. Luke's Gospel notes a song of praise called "The Magnificat" (which means magnify or exalt) that Mary declared to convey her excitement and gratitude at Jesus's coming birth (1:46-55).

The Bible also records that Mary experienced:

✳ the rejection of her son by the people who knew him best,

✳ the bloody spectacle of her son being paraded through the streets of Jerusalem with a heavy cross beam on his back, and

✳ the agonized cries of Jesus from the pain, suffering, and death on the cross.

Mary stood by him through it all. Indeed, John's Gospel says she was standing at the foot of Jesus's cross (19:25).

The famous monument showing the engagement of Mary and Joseph located in the first district of Vienna, Austria.

71 Anna, a prophetess (Luke 2)

Anna's husband died just seven years into their marriage. This devastating loss left her childless and alone.

Anna was so fervent in her devotion to God that, according to Luke 2:37, she never left the temple. She was there day and night, "worshiping with fasting and prayer night and day."

During her decades of continuous service to God, how many times did Anna intercede for Israel in prayer? How many times did she beseech the God of her people to send the long-awaited Messiah of Isaiah's prophecies? How many times did she cry out Ezekiel's prophecy for the one who would unify and protect Israel?

One day, in the twilight of her life, she saw a young couple making a purification offering at the temple after the birth of their newborn son. Anna likely had seen hundreds of newborns in the temple for purification offerings—but none like this one.

Luke 2:38 suggests that after her brief face-to-face encounter with the newborn "she began to give thanks to God and to speak of him to all who were waiting for the redemption of Jerusalem." The couple's names were Mary and Joseph. The baby's name: Jesus.

Statue of Saint Anna on the Charles Bridge in Prague, Czech Republic.

72 John the Baptist
(Matthew 3)

In the gospel narrative, John the Baptist's mandate, given by God, was to prepare the way of the Lord.

John challenged the people of Judea to turn away from sin and undergo a baptism of repentance. Hundreds of people responded—including one John didn't expect. Jesus approached John near the Jordan River and asked John to baptize him. According to Matthew, though John felt unworthy, he complied.

John confronted Herod Antipas, the ruler of Galilee, about Herod's illegal marriage to his brother's ex-wife. Herod had John arrested.

John suffered tremendously in prison—physically and spiritually. At his lowest point, he sent his disciples to Jesus to see if he was indeed the Messiah for whom Israel had been waiting. Jesus responds by describing his own ministry using phrases that evoke the messianic vision of Isaiah and other prophets of the Hebrew Bible.

Herod had conflicted emotions about John. On the one hand, he wanted to please his wife and kill him. On the other hand, he was afraid of John and he enjoyed listening to the prophet speak (Mark 6:17–20). But Herod's illegitimate wife was not so forgiving. She devised a plan and Herod had no choice but to execute the prophet.

Death only burnished John's legacy. In one of the Gospels, Jesus said, "I tell you, among those born of women none is greater than John" (Luke 7:28).

Mosaic of the baptism of Jesus Christ by Saint John the Baptist as the first Luminous mystery.

73 John
(John 19–20)

John was a fisherman from Capernaum, a blue-collar worker, like most of Jesus's other disciples. John and his brother James were nicknamed the "sons of thunder" (Mark 3:17), likely because of their fiery tempers. It was an apt moniker; according to the Gospel of Luke, John once offered to call down fire from heaven on a Samaritan village whose people refused to welcome Jesus.

John enjoyed a close relationship with Jesus as part of his inner circle. According to Matthew 17, John was present for Jesus's Transfiguration, during which the disciple heard the voice of God and saw his glory.

John maintained a fierce loyalty to Jesus. In the Gospel of Luke, Jesus put Peter and John in charge of making the arrangements for the Passover meal, which in the Synoptic Gospels (Matthew, Mark, and Luke) became the Last Supper. In the Gospel of John, when Jesus hung on the cross, one of his last acts was to entrust the "beloved disciple," who some identify as John, with the responsibility of taking care of his mother, Mary, after his death.

John emerged as one of the leaders of first-century Christianity. The book of Acts records an incident in which he and his fellow disciple Peter healed a lame man in the temple at Jerusalem.

Eventually, Peter and John were arrested and brought to the Sanhedrin (the Jewish ruling council) to defend their actions. The two were acquitted. According to Acts 4:13, "When they [the Sanhedrin] saw the boldness of Peter and John, and perceived that they were uneducated, common men, they were astonished. And they recognized that they had been with Jesus."

John is identified as a pillar of the early Christian church in Galatians 2:9. He is traditionally credited with writing the Gospel of John; 1, 2, and 3 John; and the book of Revelation. Tradition holds that John was the only apostle who did not die a martyr's death. Instead, he was exiled to the prison island of Patmos, where he lived out his final days.

Jesus, as depicted in this sculpture, with one of His apostles

74 Peter
(John 20)

Aside from Judas Iscariot, no one betrayed Jesus more egregiously than Peter. Peter was a fisherman, a rough-hewn, blue-collar type, plying his trade along the Sea of Galilee, when Jesus invited Peter and his brother Andrew to follow him. The brothers immediately left their nets and followed him.

Peter proved himself to be courageous and loyal, yet he had a tendency to speak and act hastily. His mercurial nature caused some friction in his relationship with Jesus. Yet if Peter seems to be on the receiving end of more than his share of rebukes, it may be because he dared to risk more than his fellow disciples.

During the precarious crossing of the Sea of Galilee, as described in Matthew 14, only Peter had the courage to step out of the boat in the middle of a raging storm to walk on the water toward Jesus. As recorded in the Gospel of John, on the night Jesus was arrested, only Peter dared to use his sword to protect Jesus.

Peter even showed courage by following Jesus at a distance into the high priest's courtyard. But it was here that Peter's courage evaporated. He stood in the courtyard of the high priest's residence while Jesus stood trial inside. A servant girl recognized him as a disciple of Jesus; Peter told her she was mistaken. A second person recognized him; Peter lied again about his link to Jesus. A third person recognized him as a disciple and cited his Galilean accent as proof. Peter called down curses on himself to prove that he didn't even know Jesus.

But when the crowing of the rooster signified that Jesus's prediction about Peter's denial had come true, Peter broke down in tears. But he didn't stay down long. In John 21, Jesus himself, miraculously alive after being crucified and buried, restored Peter to lead the small group of both men and women believers.

Peter became a driving force in the first-century Christian movement. He boldly proclaimed Jesus's message throughout the Jewish world—and later throughout the Gentile world—until his own death. Tradition ascribes to him the writing of 1 and 2 Peter. And one tradition says that the Gospel of Mark may be dependent on Peter's recollections of Jesus. According to church tradition, Peter was crucified upside down because he didn't believe he was worthy to be crucified in the same manner as Jesus.

75 Thomas
(John 20)

Sometimes in the Bible, a single incident is enough to tarnish an entire career. Thomas, who was also known as Didymus (perhaps because he was a twin), was one of Jesus's twelve disciples. With a few exceptions, he flies under the radar through the various Gospel narratives.

In John 11, some of Jesus's disciples expressed reluctance about returning to Judea, where an attempt had been made on Jesus's life. Thomas was the one who finally said, "Let us also go, that we may die with him" (John 11:16).

In John 14, Jesus told his followers that he was returning to heaven to prepare a place for them and that they knew the way to where he was going. Thomas sought clarification. "Lord," he said, "we do not know where you are going. How can we know the way?" (John 14:5).

Whatever his contributions were to the group dynamic of the disciples, Thomas is remembered for—and pigeonholed by—a single incident recorded in John 20. In the story, the other disciples are all abuzz about having seen Jesus—alive, following his crucifixion.

Thomas, who was absent when the first sighting took place, seemed reluctant to believe their story. In fact, he seemed to reject their eyewitness account. "Unless I see in his hands the mark of the nails, and place my finger into the mark of the nails, and place my hand into his side, I will never believe," he vowed (John 20:25). And with this statement his infamy was sealed and the idiom "doubting Thomas" was born.

Eight days later, the disciples assembled again. This time Thomas was with them. According to John 20:27, Jesus appeared once again and presented himself to Thomas for inspection. "Put your finger here, and see my hands; and put out your hand, and place it in my side. Do not disbelieve, but believe."

Before judging Thomas too harshly, we must remember that none of the other disciples initially believed Jesus was alive. They ignored the women when they reported Jesus was no longer in his tomb. According to the Gospel of John, Peter, and another disciple, whom some identify as John, part of Jesus's inner circle, ran to check out the tomb before they would believe, and the rest of the disciples believed only when Jesus suddenly appeared in their midst. But Thomas is remembered most because of his outright statement of doubt.

Thomas seems to be passionate, whether doubting or believing. Once he was sure that Jesus was alive, he responded, "My Lord and my God!" (John 20:28).

According to church tradition, Thomas later played a key role in the spread of Christianity—particularly to Persia (and perhaps even India), where he was eventually martyred for his missionary work.

DE PREDIS, Cristoforo (1440-1486). Stories of Saint Joachim, Saint Anne, Virgin Mary, Jesus, the Baptist and the End of the World. 1476. Thomas, unbelieving the resurrection of Jesus, wants to touch his side. Renaissance art. Quattrocento. Miniature Painting. ITALY. Turin. Royal Library.

76 Judas Iscariot
(Luke 22; John 12)

With a single act, Judas forever made his name synonymous with treachery and betrayal. More than 2,000 years after his death, it is still an insult to call someone a "Judas."

The origin of the name *Iscariot* is debated by Bible scholars. Some believe it comes from *Kerioth*, which may have been a region in Judea. Others believe it refers to the *sicarii*, a group of assassins who wanted to drive the Romans from Israel. And several other possible interpretations of the name exist.

Betraying Jesus was not the only black mark on Judas Iscariot's record in the Gospels. In John 12, Jesus's friend Mary pours a jar of expensive perfume on Jesus's feet and then uses her hair to wipe off the excess oil. Judas criticized her extraordinary act of generosity and service as a foolish waste of money. "Why was this ointment not sold for three hundred denarii and given to the poor?" he asked (John 12:5).

The author of the Gospel states that Judas's concerns were insincere. "He said this, not because he cared about the poor, but because he was a thief, and having charge of the moneybag he used to help himself to what was put into it" (John 12:6).

And then came the act for which Judas will forever be known. For the sum of thirty pieces of silver, Judas agreed to lead Jesus's enemies to the garden of Gethsemane, where they could arrest him.

The reasons for his betrayal are unclear in the Gospels of Mark and Matthew. The Gospels of John and Luke, says only that "Satan entered Judas called Iscariot, who was of the number of the twelve" (Luke 22:3 and similar in John 13:27)

Whatever his reasons for betraying Jesus, Judas felt only shame and regret afterward. He tried to return the money he was given, but his co-conspirators wouldn't take it back. The despondent Judas made one final decision. In the story according to Matthew 27:5, he "went and hanged himself."

Figure carved in wood of Judas Iscariot, Brotherhood of the Santa Cena Sacramental, Linares, Jaen province, Spain

(77 The Canaanite Woman
(Matthew 15)

Nevertheless, she persisted.

Almost 2,000 years before inspiring grassroots political action, the power of those words was on full display during an encounter between Jesus of Nazareth and an unnamed Canaanite woman.

To modern sensibilities, Jesus's words and actions recorded in Matthew 15 seem callous, even offensive. Yet the woman to whom they were directed would not be dissuaded in her quest.

Jesus ignored her first request: "Have mercy on me, O Lord, Son of David; my daughter is severely oppressed by a demon." His silence was so discomforting that his disciples urged him to send the woman away.

Still, she persisted—even after Jesus told her that his first priority was to help "the lost sheep of the house of Israel," and that for him to assist a Gentile would be "to take the children's bread and throw it to the dogs."

Perhaps she expected such treatment. After all, Jesus was a Jewish rabbi and she was a Gentile woman. She knew where she stood in Jewish society's pecking order.

That would explain why the Canaanite woman maintained her humble doggedness. "Yes, Lord," the woman replied, "yet even the dogs eat the crumbs that fall from their masters' table."

"O woman," Jesus said to her, "great is your faith! Be it done for you as you desire." According to Matthew 15:28, the Canaanite woman's daughter was instantly healed.

Christ and the Canaanite woman,
Pieter Lastman, 1617

78 Zacchaeus
(Luke 19)

In Jesus's day, most Jewish people despised tax collectors. From a political perspective, tax collectors were viewed as traitors for collaborating with Israel's enemies, the Romans. From a financial perspective, they were viewed as thieves who overcharged their fellow Jews and pocketed the extra money, with the approval and protection of the Roman Empire.

The Gospel of Luke introduces Zacchaeus with a single sentence: "He was a chief tax collector and was rich" (Luke 19:2).

Zacchaeus learned that Jesus of Nazareth would be passing through his city. The tax collector had an overwhelming desire to see the rabbi from Galilee who had made such a name for himself. Unfortunately, his height—or lack thereof—made it difficult for him to see over the crowd.

Zacchaeus climbed a sycamore tree. When Jesus passed by, the rabbi looked up, called Zacchaeus by name, and told him to come down so he could stay at his house that day.

Jesus's words likely sent a shock wave through the crowd, but Zacchaeus pledged to give one half of everything he owned to the poor and to repay any person he may have cheated four times the amount he took from them.

Luke 19:9–10 records Jesus's response: "Today salvation has come to this house, since he also is a son of Abraham. For the Son of Man came to seek and to save the lost."

Jesus and Zacchaeus, artist unknown

79 Martha
(Luke 10:38–42; John 11–12)

When Jesus passed through the village of Bethany, a woman named Martha welcomed him and his disciples into her home. She was a consummate hostess and made sure her visitors were served. She busied herself preparing the meal and anticipating her guests' needs.

When her sister Mary simply sat at Jesus's feet listening to his teaching while Martha bustled about, Martha said, "Lord, do you not care that my sister has left me to serve alone? Tell her then to help me" (Luke 10:40).

The teacher from Galilee reminded her of the importance of keeping her priorities straight.

"Martha, Martha," he said, "you are anxious and troubled about many things, but one thing is necessary. Mary has chosen the good portion, which will not be taken away from her" (Luke 10:41–42).

Later after Martha's brother Lazarus got sick, she and Mary sent for Jesus. But by the time Jesus got there, it was seemingly too late. Lazarus was dead, and had been in the tomb for four days. Martha demonstrated faith when she said, "But even now I know that whatever you ask from God, God will give you" (John 11:22).

And she was right. After Jesus prayed to God, he proceeded to raise Lazarus from the dead (but not before Martha warned him that surely the body would stink after four days).

In John 12, we encounter Martha a final time the same way we met her, engaged in service. Once again Jesus visited her home, and once again Martha served the guests. Once again, her sister Mary demonstrated her devotion to Jesus, but this time her display was more extravagant. She poured expensive perfume on Jesus's feet and wiped it away with her hair. While some of Jesus's disciples complained about the waste, Martha was silent.

Martha enjoyed a close relationship with Jesus. The Bible rarely shares how Jesus felt about an individual. But of this family in Bethany, John 11:5 tells us, "Now Jesus loved Martha and her sister and Lazarus."

Christ in the house of Mary and Martha, main altar in the church of Saint Matthew in Stitar, Croatia.

80 Herodias
(Mark 6:14–29)

Revenge is a dish best served cold—on a platter, in front of guests, if possible. That was the *modus operandi* of Herodias.

John the Baptist made a powerful enemy when he criticized Herod Antipas's illicit marriage to Herodias. (Herodias had left her first husband—who was Herod's half brother, no less—in order to marry the Jewish ruler of Galilee and Perea.)

Herodias bided her time planning her vengeance on the prophet.

When Herod threw a great party to impress his associates, Herodias saw her opportunity. After her daughter, Salome, had danced for the guests, Herod was so pleased with the young woman's performance that he offered to grant her any request.

The young dancer asked her mother what she should ask for, and Herodias told her to request the head of John the Baptist. Herod had no choice but to comply. To go back on his word in front of his guests would have been an embarrassment. So Herod ordered the beheading of John the Baptist, who was imprisoned. A short time later, the prophet's head was delivered to the party on a platter.

Herodias had her revenge. ·

The Dance

"For when Herodias's daughter came in and danced, she pleased Herod and his guests. And the king said to the girl, 'Ask me for whatever you wish, and I will give it to you.' " (Mark 6:23-24)

Beheading of John the Baptist by order of King Herod

81 The Faithful Centurion
(Matthew 8)

One of the most profound statements of Christian faith in the New Testament comes from an unlikely source. Jesus was walking through the fishing village of Capernaum on the northern shore of the Sea of Galilee when he encountered a Roman army officer. The centurion was a Gentile.

In the first century, Jewish people generally looked down on Gentiles—even those in Jesus's entourage. For a Gentile to approach Jesus was to risk rejection. But the centurion believed Jesus could heal his servant, who had been paralyzed by and was suffering terribly back at the centurion's house.

Jesus was moved by the man's concern for his servant and started toward his home. The centurion stopped him with these words, recorded in Matthew 8:8–9:

> "Lord, I am not worthy to have you come under my roof, but only say the word, and my servant will be healed. For I too am a man under authority, with soldiers under me. And I say to one, 'Go,' and he goes, and to another, 'Come,' and he comes, and to my servant, 'Do this,' and he does it."

In the story, Jesus told his followers that he had never seen such faith anywhere in Israel. He turned to the centurion and said, "Go; let it be done for you as you have believed." The writer of the Gospel noted that the servant was healed at that very moment.

A centurion, the Roman legionary, in an historical reconstruction of the crucifixion of Jesus Christ in the Ukraine.

82 Mary Magdalene
(John 20)

Statue of Mary Magdalene

In the wake of Jesus's arrest and crucifixion, Jesus's followers feared the Jewish religious leaders and Roman authorities. To be identified with Jesus of Nazareth was perhaps to risk a fate similar to his. His disciples scattered and hid. Only a few people dared to stay with Jesus to the bitter end.

One such person was Mary Magdalene, who had once been an outcast of society because, according to Mark and Luke, she was possessed by seven demons. According to the Gospels' narratives, Jesus had changed her life dramatically. By his authority the demons left her, and she became a new person.

She also became a faithful follower of Jesus—arguably the most loyal person in his entourage. She and a few other women traveled with Jesus.

In the Gospel of John's account of the resurrection, *one* person discovered Jesus's empty tomb. *One* person talked to the angels who were sitting inside. *One* person alerted the disciples. *One* person was the first to encounter the risen Lord.

That person was Mary Magdalene. Because she carries the good news to the other disciples, she is referenced in early and medieval Christian writings as the "apostle to the apostles."

83 Joanna
(Luke 24)

Joanna was the wife of a government official. Her husband, Chuza, managed the household of Herod Antipas, the governor of Galilee. As a prominent member of Jewish society, Joanna enjoyed a certain measure of wealth and influence.

According to the Gospel of Luke, Jesus had once healed Joanna of an unnamed affliction. Afterward, she became his devoted follower. Luke 8:3 indicates that she and others provided for Jesus of Nazareth and his disciples out of their means.

Joanna provided for Jesus and his disciples when they traveled. She made sure they were properly cared for. She even followed Jesus when he journeyed from Galilee to Jerusalem.

Her devotion to Jesus never waned, that we are told of, even after he was crucified. She was among the women, according only to Luke, who hurried to his tomb on the Sunday morning after his crucifixion to prepare his body for burial.

In the centuries that followed, the Christian church emerged as a potent force in the culture. In response, the Roman Empire sought to limit the fledgling movement's influence.

Church tradition holds that Joanna continued to support Jesus's ministry. Her influence helped guide the early church through a critical time in its development. Even the apostle Paul looked to her as a spiritual elder.

Prague, St. Vitus Cathedral, Stained Glass Window

84 Mary, the Witness to the Crucifixion
(John 19:16–25)

In ancient Rome, crucifixion was a barbaric form of execution carried out as a public spectacle. Death on a cross was the stuff of nightmares—for the prisoner, certainly, but also for those who witnessed it. The brutality of the act was reason enough for Jesus's followers to avoid Golgotha, the place of his execution.

An even more compelling reason to stay away from the scene of Jesus's death was the direction in which the political and religious winds of Jerusalem were blowing at that time. For all they knew, Jesus's followers were also being targeted for arrest and crucifixion, just as their leader was. When Jesus was arrested, Mark 14:50 records that his followers "all left him and fled."

However, "Mary, the wife of Clopas," would not be dissuaded. She stood as a witness to Jesus's execution from beginning to end.

The Bible offers little insight into her motivation. She may have felt compelled to see Jesus's ministry through to its conclusion. She may have been making sure that Jesus's body received proper burial treatment.

The Bible is also silent on what Mary's presence meant to Jesus.

Stained Glass window depicting Mary of Clopas, Mary Magdalene, Mother Mary, and Saint John the Apostle on Good Friday, in the Cathedral of Mechelen, Belgium.

85 Salome
(Matthew 20)

Discipleship should have its privileges. That's what Salome seems to have believed. Her sons James and John had been handpicked by Jesus to serve as his disciples. In time, they became something more. Along with Simon Peter, Salome's two sons became Jesus's confidants and close disciples.

Salome's request was simple, yet audacious: "Say that these two sons of mine are to sit, one at your right hand and one at your left, in your kingdom."

Jesus quickly put her ill at ease.

He replied, "You do not know what you are asking. Are you able to drink the cup that I am to drink?" They said to him, "We are able." He said to them, "You will drink my cup, but to sit at my right hand and at my left is not mine to grant, but it is for those for whom it has been prepared by my Father."

The Bible records that Salome' followed Jesus to Golgotha and witnessed his crucifixion. According to the Gospel of Luke, she was on her way to prepare Jesus's body for burial when she learned of his resurrection.

86 Herod Agrippa I
(Acts 12:1-23)

Whenever the name "Herod" appears in the Bible, you know it's not going to be good news.

The early church was just beginning to flourish, and the apostles had already begun to face persecution from the Jewish authorities. They had been arrested many times and ordered by the High Priest and the Sadducees not to preach in the name of Jesus Christ (Acts 5:17–18, 27–28, 40). However, the apostles refused to heed this order and continued to preach (Acts 5:42).

King Herod Agrippa I killed the apostle James, and when he saw that it "pleased the Jews" (Acts 12:3) he arrested Peter during the Passover and the Feast of Unleavened Bread intending to deal with him after the celebration. In the meantime, he appointed four squads of soldiers to guard Peter in the prison.

Acts 12:6-10 records that on the very night Agrippa planned to bring Peter out for sentencing, an angel appeared to Peter. He was sleeping between two soldiers when the angels woke him and instructed him to get up. When he did, the chains fell from his hands, and as they left, the gates of the city opened of their own accord.

In the morning, the soldiers panicked when they realized Peter was gone and they couldn't determine what had happened to him. Herod Agrippa searched for Peter as well and couldn't find him. When he questioned the guards and received no answers, he had them executed.

Later, Agrippa left Judea and went to Caesarea to meet with the people of Tyre and Sidon. He had been angry with them, but they had requested terms of peace. Agrippa sat on the throne wearing his royal robes and addressed the people. In response, they flattered him by identifying him as a god. Acts 12:23 states, "Immediately an angel of the Lord struck him down, because he did not give God the glory, and he was eaten by worms and breathed his last."

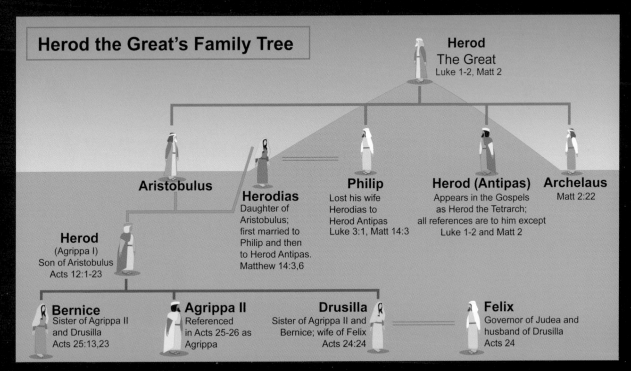

Herod the Great's Family Tree

Herod The Great
Luke 1-2, Matt 2

Aristobulus

Herodias
Daughter of Aristobulus; first married to Philip and then to Herod Antipas.
Matthew 14:3,6

Philip
Lost his wife Herodias to Herod Antipas
Luke 3:1, Matt 14:3

Herod (Antipas)
Appears in the Gospels as Herod the Tetrarch; all references are to him except Luke 1-2 and Matt 2

Archelaus
Matt 2:22

Herod
(Agrippa I)
Son of Aristobulus
Acts 12:1-23

Bernice
Sister of Agrippa II and Drusilla
Acts 25:13,23

Agrippa II
Referenced in Acts 25-26 as Agrippa

Drusilla
Sister of Agrippa II and Bernice; wife of Felix
Acts 24:24

Felix
Governor of Judea and husband of Drusilla
Acts 24

(87) Barnabas
(Acts 4–19)

Joseph from Cyprus, a first-century Levite and follower of Jesus, was nicknamed Barnabas (meaning "son of encouragement") by the apostles. Barnabas recognized potential in a new Christian convert named Paul (formerly Saul). Not only did he introduce Paul to the apostles after his conversion, but he also recruited Paul to help him teach at the church in Antioch. So began one of the most prominent partnerships in Christian history.

Yet Barnabas was more than just a perceptive judge of talent and character. He was also known for his generosity and encouraging nature. When a famine threatened the lives of Christians in Judea, the church in Antioch sent aid to their fellow believers. They put Barnabas and Paul in charge of delivering that aid.

Afterward, the church in Antioch commissioned Barnabas and Paul to embark upon a mission to Cyprus. John Mark, a relative of Barnabas's, started the journey with them, but he eventually abandoned them to return home. Barnabas and Paul preached in Lystra, Iconium, and Derbe. They found support and opposition in equal measure.

Barnabas appeared with Paul before the Jerusalem Council to argue for the full admission of Gentiles into the church. Their words went a long way toward resolving the ongoing controversy.

When the time came to launch a second missionary journey, Barnabas wanted to include John Mark again. Paul was less keen on giving the young man a second chance. The two missionaries disagreed so sharply over the matter that they decided to part ways. Each man continued his missionary work with a new partner.

Barnabas all but disappears from the New Testament narrative after that. However, Paul did offer a postscript of sorts. As the end of his life neared, Paul seems to have reconciled with John Mark. It seems Barnabas's patience and faith in the young man paid off.

Monastery of St. Barnabas, Northern Cyprus

88 Sapphira
(Acts 5:1-11)

Sacrifice and generosity were cornerstones of the early Christian church. Acts 2 records that members often pooled their resources in order to provide for everyone. A Christian leader named Barnabas (the future traveling companion of the apostle Paul) set a standard for generosity when he sold land that he owned and gave the money to the apostles to help care for the poor.

Like Barnabas, Sapphira and Ananias sold a piece of property they owned and laid the proceeds at the apostles' feet. *Most* of the proceeds, that is. Unlike Barnabas, they held back a portion of the profits to line their own pockets. But they let everyone believe they had given it all, just as Barnabas had done.

Sapphira wasn't present when her husband made his presentation to the apostles. She showed up three hours later. She was greeted with a simple request by the apostle Peter: "Tell me whether you sold the land for so much."

The Bible doesn't say whether Sapphira weighed the pros and cons of answering truthfully. She certainly didn't understand what was at stake. She couldn't see the body of her husband, who had been struck dead by God for lying to the Holy Spirit.

"Yes," she lied about the sale price, "for so much." The Bible says that immediately after she spoke those untruthful words, she fell to the floor and died. As a result, "great fear came upon the whole church and upon all who heard of these things."

'The Death of Sapphira', 1654-1656, Oil on canvas. Nicolas Poussin (1594-1665) French painter. Ananias and his wife Sapphira.

89 Stephen
(Acts 6-7)

Stephen is the first person in the New Testament to face martyrdom. He rose to prominence in the first-century church as a man of unimpeachable reputation.

When a dispute arose regarding the treatment of Greek widows in the church, the twelve apostles stepped in to arbitrate. The apostles recommended appointing seven men who were "full of the Spirit and of wisdom" to oversee the distribution of food (Acts 6:3). Stephen was one of the seven men chosen for the task.

Stephen also carved out a reputation for himself as a powerful evangelist. Acts 6:8 suggests that his words were accompanied by great wonders and signs. Not surprisingly, the Bible states that Stephen drew opposition from religious authorities who were keen to see the fledgling Christian movement fail. These opponents were not above instigating false testimony to achieve their goals.

According to the Bible, Stephen was accused of blasphemy "against Moses and God" (Acts 6:11). Rabble-rousers turned public sentiment against him. Stephen was arrested and brought before the Jewish council (Sanhedrin). His accusers demanded that he answer the charges against him. Instead, Stephen launched into the longest sermon in the book of Acts. He spoke of Jewish history, God's covenant with Israel, and Israel's rejection of the long-awaited Messiah. He spoke of the tabernacle and the temple.

Stephen ended his sermon with a rebuke of his accusers. He called them "stiff-necked people" who resisted the Holy Spirit (Acts 7:51). He accused them of killing God's prophets—and of betraying and murdering Jesus.

That was all his accusers could stand. They seized Stephen, dragged him outside the city, and stoned him to death. Stephen became the first Christian martyr in the Bible.

Statue of St. Stephen. St. Stephen's Cathedral

90 Saul of Tarsus
(Acts 7:58 – 9:43)

An angry mob dragged Stephen to a place outside Jerusalem, furious at his accusations. According to Jewish regulations, a convicted criminal needed to be taken outside the city and placed, often thrown, into a hole at least twice the person's height. Several priests and elders removed their cloaks for the task they were about to undergo.

The witnesses left their outer garments with a young man. He witnessed the push that sent Stephen over the precipice and onto the rocks below. He listened to Stephen's death throes as large stones were dropped onto his helpless and prone body. And he approved of it all. The book of Acts doesn't elaborate on what role he played in Stephen's execution, but it does single him out by name—"a young man named Saul" (Acts 7:58).

Stephen's execution initiated a wide scale persecution of Jesus's followers, and afterward Saul launched his own campaign of terror and intimidation against them. He soon had a reputation in and around Jerusalem as one of the most dangerous enemies of believers who belonged to "the Way" (Acts 9:1–2, 13–14).

Saul was driven by his passion for the Torah. He saw the subversive following that sprang up around Jesus of Nazareth as a challenge to the true Law, and he was determined to stamp out the movement before it grew more popular. In addition to his unimpeachable Jewish training and knowledge (Acts 22:3), Saul also had a coveted Roman citizenship (Acts 22:27–28). The terror he inspired in those he considered blasphemers was well earned.

According to Jewish law, people accused of blasphemy had to stand trial before the Sanhedrin, which met in the temple complex of Jerusalem. When Saul heard of potential members of the Way in Damascus, he volunteered to travel the 150 miles and haul any he found back to Jerusalem. The high priest gave him the authority to do so. As Saul neared Damascus, he was probably convinced that nothing could deter him from completing his mission.

He was wrong.

Statue of St. Paul with book and sword, from Santa Maria Assunta Jesuit church facade in Venice (18th century)

91 Paul
(Acts 9:1-19; 22:2-16; 26:9-18)

Jesus was dead —at least, that was the story being perpetrated by the Jewish religious leaders. Jesus's followers knew better. Their numbers were growing rapidly. But one of their leaders, the servant Stephen, had become too outspoken before the Sanhedrin. His boldness resulted in his immediate execution, followed by a widespread persecution of other believers. People were being murdered and put in prison for their beliefs.

One of the most determined persecutors was Saul of Tarsus. He secured permission from the high priest to travel to Damascus, arrest any Jesus followers he found there, and extradite them back to Jerusalem for trial.

Just before he arrived in Damascus Saul was blinded by a heavenly light and heard a voice, one identified as "Jesus, whom you are persecuting." Still unable to see, he had to be led into Damascus.

Once Saul became convinced he had met the resurrected Jesus, his fervor was redirected into the *growth* of the church. He was a Roman citizen, a rarity among Jesus's earliest followers. As such, he enjoyed privileges that other leaders of the movement did not and he recognized the importance of welcoming and even recruiting Gentiles to the cause. He soon became better known by his Latin name, Paul.

Paul was fearless in his preaching of Jesus' message—and bold in his ambition to spread it. The book of Acts records three of his missionary journeys. The first he took with his companion, Barnabas—a Jew from Cyprus. Traveling by sea and by land through the Roman Empire, they went first to Cyprus and then continued to the cities of Asia Minor. Paul's strategy was to focus on the large urban centers, first visiting the local synagogue to present his message to the Jews, then (often after being rejected) turning to the non-Jewish population. His message wasn't always well-received; at one point on this journey he was stoned and left for dead.

During his second journey, he and his companion Silas were beaten and thrown in prison in Philippi. An earthquake opened their cell doors and freed them from their chains, but the missionaries refused to escape. Their jailer was so moved by their gesture that he and his entire household believed in Paul's God and were baptized.

During his third journey, Paul healed a young man who was thought to be dead. He also narrowly escaped a riot in Ephesus. The journey ended in Jerusalem, where Paul was beaten by a Jewish mob, arrested, and taken into protective custody by Roman soldiers.

The biblical account of Paul's life ends as he is awaiting trial. Church tradition suggests that he spent years as a prisoner in Rome before he was beheaded around AD 67.

Although not one of Jesus's original Twelve, Paul considered himself an *apostle* because he saw Jesus and was called by him into an extraordinary life. It was a title that both honored and humbled him throughout his long and faithful ministry (1 Corinthians 15:7-9).

Saint Paul Statue in Rome

The Conversion of St. Paul fresco in Cathedral of Assumption of the Blessed Virgin Mary by unknown artist (1811), Cremona, Italy.

The Surprise Twist

The villainous Saul of Tarsus (see page 99) and the heroic apostle Paul were the same person! Yet the change that took place was dramatic enough to posit that the before-conversion Saul and the after-conversion Paul were two different people.

In Acts 9, the New Testament attributes the astonishing transformation to an encounter with the risen Jesus. Saul was on his way to Damascus to arrest Christians when a bright light knocked him to the ground and left him temporarily blinded.

"Saul, Saul, why do you persecute me?" a voice called.

"Who are you, Lord?" Saul asked.

"I am Jesus, whom you are persecuting," the voice replied. "Now get up and go into the city, and you will be told what you must do" (Acts 9:4-6).

In Damascus, a Christian named Ananias met him. "Placing his hands on Saul, he said, 'Brother Saul, the Lord—Jesus, who appeared to you on the road as you were coming here—has sent me so that you might see again and be filled with the Holy Spirit.' Immediately, something like scales fell from Saul's eyes, and he could see again. He got up and was baptized" (Acts 9:17-18).

A short time later, Paul started teaching about Jesus in the local synagogues. His fellow Christians were understandably skeptical about this change in him at first. Even the apostles were reluctant to embrace him. In time, though, people recognized that his transformation was real.

92 Philip
(Acts 8)

An Ethiopian court official was returning home from worshiping in Jerusalem when he stopped his chariot beside the road in Gaza and started reading the book of Isaiah.

A man approached his chariot. "Do you understand what you are reading?" the man asked (Acts 8:30).

"How can I, unless someone guides me?" the Ethiopian replied (Acts 8:31).

The man who approached the chariot was Philip, who, according to Acts 8:26, had been instructed by an angel of the Lord to leave Jerusalem and head for Gaza.

Along with Stephen, who became the first Christian martyr, Philip had been chosen to fill a key leadership role in the fledgling Christian movement. He oversaw the distribution of food to those who needed it and made sure no one was overlooked in the process.

The Ethiopian invited Philip onto his chariot. While they rode together, Philip explained that Jesus of Nazareth had fulfilled the prophecy in Isaiah that the Ethiopian had had trouble understanding. Acts 8:35 says Philip told the man "the good news about Jesus."

The Ethiopian was so moved that he stopped his chariot beside a body of water and asked Philip to baptize him on the spot. Acts 8:39 ends the story with the supernatural: "And when they came up out of the water, the Spirit of the Lord carried Philip away, and the eunuch saw him no more, and went on his way rejoicing."

Philip's act of kindness may have had far-reaching effects. Ethiopian tradition holds that Christianity spread to Ethiopia due to the influence of the Ethiopian official Philip tutored.

Saint Philip the Apostle. El Greco, Dominico (1541-1614)

93 Dorcas
(Acts 9)

One person's death can deeply affect those who loved and knew them. Such was the case in the bizarre story told in Acts 9, when Dorcas (also known as Tabitha) died.

The story doesn't say how Dorcas died, but it does describe how her death affected others.

The widows who came to mourn carried with them garments that Dorcas had made for them. The fact that Dorcas made garments for widows suggests that she may have been a widow herself. In first-century Jewish culture, some widows helped take care of those in need.

According to Acts 9, word circulated among the disciples, who sent men to alert Peter, who was nearby. Two men were dispatched to fetch him. When Peter arrived, he cleared the room. He then prayed over Dorcas's body and told her to get up. The Bible tells us "she opened her eyes, and when she saw Peter, she sat up."

The Miracle

"So Peter rose and went with them. And when he arrived, they took him to the upper room. All the widows stood beside him weeping and showing tunics and other garments that Dorcas made while she was with them. But Peter put them all outside, and knelt down and prayed; and turning to the body he said, "Tabitha, arise." And she opened her eyes, and when she saw Peter she sat up. And he gave her his hand and raised her up. Then, calling the saints and widows, he presented her alive" (Acts 39-41)

A stained glass window depicting the story of Dorcas, or Tabitha (Acts 9:36-42)

103

94 Cornelius
(Acts 10)

Gentiles were considered second-class citizens in the early days of the first-century church. Many Jewish followers of Jesus—including church leaders—struggled to overcome their cultural bias against people from other nations.

One of the first Gentile converts to Christianity was a Roman centurion named Cornelius. He was a man of strong character, known especially for his generosity and his commitment to prayer. According to Acts 10, an angel of the Lord appeared to Cornelius one day and instructed him to send for the apostle Peter.

Cornelius was so overwhelmed that Peter accepted his invitation that he fell down and tried to worship the apostle. Peter quickly pulled him to his feet and reminded Cornelius that he was just a man. Cornelius's excitement was understandable. Peter's willingness to enter his home was almost unprecedented. Jewish people—especially Jewish people of Peter's status—simply didn't go into the homes of Gentiles.

Cornelius had invited his family and close friends to hear Peter speak in his home. The apostle didn't disappoint. He told the gathered crowd about Jesus and acknowledged that the church should show no partiality toward anyone.

The narrative of Acts 10 suggests that the Holy Spirit descended on the Gentiles in Cornelius's home, just as he had done with the disciples at Pentecost.

The baptism of St. Cornelius the Centurion, 17th century

(95) John Mark
(Acts 13)

John Mark's family was well known in first-century Christian circles. His mother was a woman named Mary who opened her home as a meeting place for the early church. The apostle Peter spent time in their home. John Mark was the younger cousin of Barnabas, the traveling companion of the apostle Paul.

That might explain why John Mark (also called Mark) was invited to accompany Paul and Barnabas on their first missionary journey. Acts 13:5 describes his role as an assistant. But at one point he left them in Perga and returned to Jerusalem. Sometime later, when Paul and Barnabas were preparing for their second missionary journey, Barnabas suggested taking John Mark with them again. Paul opposed the idea. Their disagreement led to the two of them parting ways. Paul teamed with Silas for his next journey; Barnabas traveled to Cyprus with John Mark.

Though we don't know the details, Mark later reconciled with Paul (Colossians 4:10, Philemon 24). In 2 Timothy 4:11, Paul states that Mark "is very useful to me for ministry."

Peter refers to Mark as his "son" in 1 Peter 5:13. Tradition holds that Mark was Peter's assistant and that he wrote down Peter's recollections of Jesus for the second Gospel, Mark, which Christian tradition attributes to him.

Statue of Mark the Evangelist with the lion inside the Sanctuary of the Madonna di San Luca, a basilica church in Bologna, northern Italy.

96 Lydia
(Acts 16)

Lydia was a successful businesswoman who dealt in expensive purple cloth. Her clients were the power players of first-century society. She was comfortable doing business with Jews and also with Gentiles, like herself.

According to Acts 16, Lydia became a follower of Jesus after listening to the apostle Paul speak about Jesus.

After she and her family were baptized, Lydia extended an offer of hospitality to Paul and his companions.

In the end, Paul accepted Lydia's invitation. "And after she was baptized, and her household as well, she urged us, saying, "If you have judged me to be faithful to the Lord, come to my house and stay." And she prevailed upon us." (Acts 16:15).

Above: Traditional location of Lydia's baptism in Philippi (Greece).

(97 Silas
(Acts 16–17)

Also known as Silvanus, Silas was one of the most trusted leaders in the early church. When a controversial teaching that required Gentiles to be circumcised before they could be baptized threatened to divide the church, Silas was one of the men chosen to help repair the rift (Acts 15:22).

Silas was possibly a Roman citizen, like Paul, which gave him more freedom and privileges than most of the other early Jewish Christians. He likely was also highly educated. Many scholars believe he helped write 1 and 2 Thessalonians and 1 Peter.

Silas became Paul's traveling companion for the apostle's second missionary journey, after Paul's falling out with Barnabas. In Philippi, the two men ministered to the Jewish population until they were arrested as revolutionaries. According to Acts 16, the two men were freed from their chains by an earthquake. Out of respect for their jailer, however, Paul and Silas didn't leave the jail. They remained there with the other prisoners. The jailer was so moved by their gesture that he converted to Christianity.

Silas moved on with Paul to strengthen and encourage Christian congregations in Thessalonica, Berea, and Corinth.

This is the agora in Philippi where Paul and Silas would have visited before being thrown in jail.

(98 Priscilla
(Romans 16)

The apostle Paul and other leaders of the first-century church were able to do what they did because they had the support and assistance of Priscilla and others like her.

Priscilla likely was among the first Christian converts in Rome. When Emperor Claudius expelled all Jews from the capital city, she and her husband, Aquila, relocated to Corinth.

Like the apostle Paul, Priscilla and Aquila were tentmakers by profession. That may explain why the apostle made a point of visiting them when he traveled to Corinth. He ended up staying and working with the couple for an extended time. When he finally sailed to Syria, he took Priscilla and Aquila with him.

Along the way, the three of them decided that Priscilla and Aquila's ministry gifts were most needed in the city of Ephesus. According to Acts, while in Ephesus they encountered Apollos, who boldly proclaimed the message of Jesus in the synagogue. The married duo noticed that Apollos's knowledge of certain Christian doctrines was limited, so they took him home and tutored him.

The reference to the couple in Romans 16:3–4 is especially telling: "Greet Priscilla and Aquila, my fellow workers in Christ Jesus. They risked their lives for me. Not only I but all the churches of the Gentiles are grateful to them." 1 Corinthians 16:19 reveals that they opened up their home to serve as a church.

Christian tradition holds that they ultimately laid down their lives for Jesus's sake. The eighth of July is the day set apart for them in the martyrology of the Roman Catholic Church, when it is said the faithful couple were led out beyond the walls and beheaded.

St. Aquila and his wife, St. Priscilla.

99 Timothy
(2 Timothy 2)

In 2 Timothy 2:15, the writer cites Timothy's strong Christian faith as having been influenced by the faith of his mother, Eunice, and his grandmother, Lois.

Paul met Timothy during a visit to Lystra on his second missionary journey. Before long, the two were traveling companions and coworkers. Paul looked to Timothy as his son in the Christian faith. He entrusted the young man with important missions. Around AD 64, Paul arranged for Timothy to lead the church at Ephesus. Timothy may have been considerably younger than many people in his congregation, since Paul urged him not to let anyone look down on him because of his youth.

In the epistle of 2 Timothy, which some scholars consider to be written by Paul from prison while he was awaiting trial, the apostle hints at the loneliness and isolation he was feeling. Paul knew the end of his life was near, and he longed to see his closest friends one last time. In his previous letters, Paul had mentioned a variety of friends and coworkers, some of whom stayed faithful to him and his ministry and others of whom drifted away.

In the end, though, Paul needed just three faithful friends: Luke, Mark, and Timothy.

The theater in Ephesus. Timothy was the leader of the church in this important city.

Marble statue of Moses sculpted by Michelangelo in the San Pietro in Vincoli church in Rome, Italy

ART CREDITS

museum of the Bible

Experience the Book that Shapes History

Museum of the Bible is a 430,000-square-foot building located in the heart of Washington, D.C.—just steps from the National Mall and the U.S. Capitol. Displaying artifacts from several collections, the Museum explores the Bible's history, narrative and impact through high-tech exhibits, immersive settings, and interactive experiences. At the entrance are two massive, bronze gates with Genesis 1 in Latin, as found in the Gutenberg Bible. Beyond the gates, an incredible replica of an ancient artifact containing Psalm 19 hangs behind etched glass panels. Come be inspired by the imagination and innovation used to display thousands of years of biblical history.

Museum of the Bible aims to be the most technologically advanced museum in the world, starting with its unique Digital Guide that allows guests to personalize their museum experience with navigation, customized tours, supplemental visual and audio content, and more.

For more information and to plan your visit, go to museumoftheBible.org.

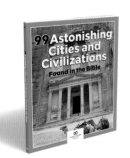

Complete Your Collection

To find more books in this series, visit: museumoftheBibleBooks.com